STEWARDSHIP OF THE SINGAPORE MEDIA

STAYING THE COURSE

IPS-NATHAN LECTURES

STEWARDSHIP OF THE SINGAPORE MEDIA

STAYING THE COURSE

PATRICK DANIEL

Published by

World Scientific Publishing Co. Pte. Ltd.
5 Toh Tuck Link, Singapore 596224
USA office: 27 Warren Street, Suite 401-402, Hackensack, NJ 07601
UK office: 57 Shelton Street, Covent Garden, London WC2H 9HE

National Library Board, Singapore Cataloguing in Publication Data
Name(s): Daniel, Patrick, 1954– | Institute of Policy Studies (Singapore)
Title: Stewardship of the Singapore media : staying the course / Patrick Daniel.
Other Title(s): IPS-Nathan Lecture series.
Description: Singapore : World Scientific Publishing Co. Pte. Ltd., [2023]
Identifier(s): ISBN 978-981-12-6830-4 (hardcover) | 978-981-12-6943-1 (paperback) |
    978-981-12-6831-1 (ebook for institutions) | 978-981-12-6832-8 (ebook for individuals)
Subject(s): LCSH: Mass media--Singapore--History. | Mass media--Singapore--21st century.
Classification: DDC 302.23095957--dc23

British Library Cataloguing-in-Publication Data
A catalogue record for this book is available from the British Library.

Copyright © 2023 by Patrick Daniel & Institute of Policy Studies, National University of Singapore

All rights reserved.

For any available supplementary material, please visit
https://www.worldscientific.com/worldscibooks/10.1142/13199#t=suppl

Desk Editor: Lai Ann

Typeset by Stallion Press
Email: enquiries@stallionpress.com

THE S R NATHAN FELLOWSHIP FOR THE STUDY OF SINGAPORE

AND THE IPS-NATHAN LECTURE SERIES

The S R Nathan Fellowship for the Study of Singapore was established by the Institute of Policy Studies (IPS) in 2013 to support research on public policy and governance issues. With the generous contributions of individual and corporate donors, and a matching government grant, IPS raised around S$5.9 million to endow the Fellowship.

Each S R Nathan Fellow, appointed under the Fellowship, delivers a series of IPS-Nathan Lectures during his or her term. These public lectures aim to promote public understanding and discourse on issues of critical national interest.

The Fellowship is named after Singapore's sixth and longest-serving President, the late S R Nathan, in recognition of his lifetime of service to Singapore.

IPS-Nathan Lectures

Print ISSN: 2630-4996
Online ISSN: 2630-5003

Published

Vol. 11: *Stewardship of the Singapore Media: Staying the Course*
by Patrick Daniel

Vol. 10: *Singapore and Multilateral Governance: Securing Our Future*
by Noeleen Heyzer

Vol. 9: *The Singapore Synthesis: Innovation, Inclusion, Inspiration*
by Ravi Menon

Vol. 8: *Gender Equality: The Time Has Come*
by Corinna Lim

Vol. 7: *World in Transition: Singapore's Future*
by Chan Heng Chee

Vol. 6: *The Idea of Singapore: Smallness Unconstrained*
by Tan Tai Yong

Vol. 5: *Seeking a Better Urban Future*
by Cheong Koon Hean

Vol. 4: *Can Singapore Fall?: Making the Future for Singapore*
by Lim Siong Guan

Vol. 3: *The Challenges of Governance in a Complex World*
by Peter Ho

Vol. 2: *Dealing with an Ambiguous World*
by Bilahari Kausikan

Vol. 1: *The Ocean in a Drop Singapore: The Next Fifty Years*
by Ho Kwong Ping

CONTENTS

Foreword — ix
About the Moderators — xvii
About the Illustrator — xviii

Lecture I — The Singapore Media's Long and Winding Road: 1824 to 2022 — 1

    Part I: Press Freedom vs Regulation — 3
    Part II: Looking Back at The History — 15
    Part III: The Last Two Decades — 29
    Question-and-Answer Session — 36
    Moderator: Professor Chan Heng Chee

Lecture II — Grappling with the Darker Side of the Internet: A Global Challenge — 47

    Part I: The Phenomenal Impact of the Internet — 49
    Part II: The Darker Side of the Internet — 56
    Part III: What is the Way Forward for Internet Governance? — 64
    Question-and-Answer Session — 68
    Moderator: Dr Carol Soon

Lecture III — Envisioning Desired Futures for Singapore and for the Local Media   **79**
   Backcasting vs Forecasting   81
   Desired Futures for Singapore   83
   Desired Futures for the Singapore Media   97
   Question-and-Answer Session   102
   Moderator: Dr Shashi Jayakumar

Bibliography   **111**
Index   **121**

FOREWORD

Mr Patrick Daniel speaking at the first lecture of his IPS-Nathan Lecture series
Source: Jacky Ho for the Institute of Policy Studies

I must thank the Institute of Policy Studies and in particular Janadas Devan, its director and my former colleague at *The Straits Times* (*ST*), for the honour of being the 11th S R Nathan Fellow.

It is especially meaningful to me because the late Mr Nathan played a big part in my joining *ST* in October 1986 as a senior writer.

I want to first pay a tribute to "SR", as we referred to him then. The story of his entering the newspaper world is actually a fitting foreword for my lecture series on the Singapore media.

Tribute to S R Nathan

SR was Executive Chairman of Straits Times Press (1975) Ltd, or STP, for six years from February 1982 to April 1988. He was sent there by Mr Lee Kuan Yew, the Prime Minister then, at the request of two top STP executives, Peter Lim, the Editor-in-Chief, and Lyndley Holloway, the Managing Director. (This was prior to SR serving two terms as the sixth President of Singapore and his two earlier postings as High Commissioner to Malaysia and Ambassador to the United States.)

SR wrote about his newspaper stint in his memoirs, *An Unexpected Journey: Path to the Presidency*. Here is how he recollected his meeting with Mr Lee in January 1982 before he took up his new appointment upon retiring from the Singapore civil service:

> *As I walked to the door (after the meeting), the Prime Minister called me back.*
>
> *I remember his words: "Nathan — I am giving you The Straits Times. It has 150 years of history. It has been a good paper. It is like a bowl of china. If you break it, I can piece it together. But it will never be the same. Try not to destroy it."*
>
> *I said nothing. He said: "You are keeping silent."*
>
> *I said, "Sir, you have told me what to do. Also what I should not do. What is there for me to say? I'll try."*
>
> *And so I left.*[1]

There is much that can be read into this quote. But clearly, it was not an assignment SR relished. By his own admission, he had no newspaper experience and was entering an altogether different world. Prior to this, he had been First Permanent Secretary in the Ministry of Foreign Affairs and Director of the Security and Intelligence Division, the foreign intelligence service under the Ministry of Defence.

---

[1] S. R. Nathan, *An Unexpected Journey: Path to the Presidency* (Singapore: Editions Didier Millet Pte Ltd, 2011), 458.

Not surprisingly, SR initially had a difficult time establishing rapport with *ST* editors and journalists. However, he used his considerable skills, charm and patience to win them over. He decided early to "lead from the rear" and made his mark in several areas.[2] The first was the immediate task of repairing the strained relationship between editors and the Lee Kuan Yew government. SR achieved this without interfering in daily news operations.

Next, he impressed upon editors the need to actively scout for talent. He also used his wide network to establish learning programmes for journalists and editors. A signature early programme was the short sabbaticals he arranged at Wolfson College in Cambridge University. In my case, he arranged a three-month attachment at the *Financial Times*, which I enjoyed and learnt a great deal from.

SR's chairmanship included a major corporate restructuring of the Singapore media, driven by Mr Lee, which I recount in my first lecture. SR's memoirs on this make sad reading as he was not privy to the discussions on the merger of Singapore's two rival newspaper groups and the formation of Singapore Press Holdings (SPH) in 1984. He wrote:

> *I felt let down that the people at the top had ... kept me out of the loop. In the circumstances I decided to let it be known that I would like to step down.*[3]

But SR stayed on till April 1988, shortly after turning down a belated offer to be CEO of SPH when Lyndley Holloway left the group. Cheong Yip Seng, Editor-in-Chief at the time, spoke for many when he wrote to SR in a farewell note:

> *When you first came, many journalists were hostile. When you left, we all felt a deep sense of loss. You earned our respect .... No*

---

[2] Ibid., 463.
[3] Ibid., 492.

chief executive since your time has given editorial the same level of personal attention.[4]

I was not yet in *ST* during SPH's early years. My first dealing with *ST* was in mid-1986 when I was in the Ministry of Trade and Industry (MTI). I was Secretary to the Economic Committee which Lee Hsien Loong, or BG Lee as he was known then, chaired as Minister of State.

When the report was released, I was invited by *ST* to brief their journalists on the report's recommendations. I must have done a half-decent job because shortly after, SR asked Peter Lim to entice me with an offer to join the paper. I declined twice, as I was enjoying the work in MTI, but they sweetened the offer until I eventually agreed. This was a time when the civil service paid low salaries.

When SR heard I was worried that Ngiam Tong Dow, my Permanent Secretary at MTI whom I had great respect for, might stop me from leaving, he spoke directly with BG Lee. One morning, BG Lee said to me after a meeting: "I hear *ST* wants to hire you. Think carefully. It is a slippery totem pole you have to climb."

I recount this really to pay a heartfelt tribute to SR for my career switch to journalism. I consider myself truly fortunate, as I found a profession that suited me so well. This is why I stayed for more than 30 years. When you love what you do, time flies. This is also why it did not take me long to say yes when Janadas approached me to be a Nathan Fellow.

Telling the Singapore Media Story

A bigger factor in my decision to accept Janadas' invite was that the Singapore media, and in particular SPH, was at the cusp of yet another major transformation, which I could put into perspective. SPH, a listed company then, announced in June 2021 that it would spin off its media operations to a new not-for-profit entity, the SPH Media Trust. I had retired in August 2018 but was persuaded to return as Interim CEO of the new entity.

---

[4] Ibid., 493.

In fact, a year earlier in July 2020, at the 175th anniversary of *ST*, I was invited by the newspaper to provide a quote as a retired former editor-in-chief. This is what I said:

> *The days when ST enjoyed profit margins above 30 per cent are gone — savaged by technology platforms which have sucked up the bulk of advertising revenues. I'm convinced that newspapers have to find a new ownership model to survive — either be owned by a billionaire or convert to a public trust. I much prefer the latter, and predict ST will go that way and live to celebrate its 200th anniversary.*[5]

I had no idea then that conversion to a trust would come to pass, and so soon. I did float this proposal to SPH management before I retired, but it was not taken up and I thought the idea was dead in the water. When it did come to life, I knew that the story of Singapore's media would make a good topic for an IPS-Nathan lecture series.

Outline of Lecture I — The Singapore Media's Long and Winding Road: 1824 to 2022

As I conceptualised my lectures, I felt I must recount the Singapore legacy media's long history since the colonial era. This would put into context the key issues at the heart of the Lee Kuan Yew government's post-Independence approach to press freedom and media regulation, through laws like the Newspaper and Printing Presses Act and the Broadcasting Act.

I also wanted to trace the almost-forgotten government crackdowns against several media titles in the 1970s, as well as its active stewardship role in the 1980s in reshaping the media landscape to ensure that vernacular papers survived.

---

[5] Shefali Rekhi, "ST Turns 175: Previous Editors on the Paper's Place in Society," *The Straits Times*, July 15, 2020, https://www.straitstimes.com/singapore/st175-previous-editors-on-st.

The latest turn in this long road has come after two decades of disruption by the Internet giants. Not surprisingly, the decision by the government to provide funding support to the new not-for-profit entity immediately raised many questions: Is taxpayer support justified? And how will government funding affect the media's independence? These are questions I wanted to address.

Outline of Lecture II — Grappling With the Darker Side of the Internet: A Global Challenge

For my second lecture, I felt I must cover the rise of the Internet — arguably the most far-reaching invention the world has seen. Since its origins in the 1960s, the Internet revolution has taken human communication to an altogether new level for billions of people. For businesses, including the media, it has brought a whirlwind of benefits, but also challenges.

I have chosen to focus on the challenges, in particular the Internet's darker side — everything from wilful misinformation to online fraud. I use as a case study the US$600 billion global digital advertising ecosystem at the heart of the Internet.

The larger question I wanted to pose is: After decades of a light-touch regime, has the time come for more effective global governance of the Internet? Or are regulators too far behind the curve? How this plays out will have a big impact on societies everywhere, as well as on business enterprises, including the media.

Outline of Lecture III — Envisioning Desired Futures for Singapore and for the Local Media

For my final lecture, I hoped to look into the future. As a country, Singapore will have to contend with a slew of polarising issues in the years ahead — everything from geopolitics and domestic income inequality to the global climate crisis and accelerating technological advances such as artificial intelligence.

But rather than try to forecast Singapore's future trajectories, I decided to take an alternative approach called "backcasting". The idea is to envision feasible desired futures for key aspects of our society, and then "backcast" or look back to the present to decide what policies are needed to attain those desired futures.

My lecture series concludes by looking at the desired future for the local news media, in particular the SPH Media Trust. It addresses the question: What are the steps it must take to get to its desired future?

Acknowledgements

When I took up the challenge of doing my three lectures, I did not imagine how much reading and research it would entail. I wish I could have had more time to consult with more colleagues and friends to sharpen my points and add polish to my lectures. But being the journalist that I am, I finalised my lectures just before delivering them. Notwithstanding this, I must thank several people for helping me pull this off:

— Liang Kaixin and her diligent team at IPS for their help and efficient arrangements. In particular, I thank Latasha Seow, my bright young research assistant who was a pleasure to work with.

— Professor Chan Heng Chee, Dr Carol Soon and Dr Shashi Jayakumar for the excellent job they did moderating the question-and-answer sessions that followed each of my lectures.

— My former colleagues in SPH, as well as in the wider Singapore media industry, for the fulfilling career I have enjoyed. I have learnt so much and owe them all a debt of gratitude.

— My family, especially my wife whose help and incisive comments on my lectures were invaluable.

I dedicate this book to my beloved parents, especially my mother who passed away in February 2020 at the age of 94. Their decision to leave their ancestral home in Kerala, India and sink roots in Singapore has made me the person that I am.

Patrick Daniel
August 2022

Post-script (14 January 2023): My three lectures, delivered in early 2022, did not capture the recent revelations of overstatement of SPH Media's circulation numbers. PD

ABOUT THE MODERATORS

Professor Chan Heng Chee is Ambassador-at-Large at the Ministry of Foreign Affairs and Professor at the Lee Kuan Yew Centre for Innovative Cities at the Singapore University of Technology and Design. Ambassador Chan is Chairman of the Board of Trustees at ISEAS-Yusof Ishak Institute (ISEAS), Deputy Chairman of the Social Science Research Council, and Global Co-Chair of Asia Society. She is a member of the Science of Cities Committee (National Research Foundation), the Board of Trustees of the National University of Singapore, the Yale-NUS Governing Board and the Presidential Council for Minority Rights. In August 2022, she was appointed to the Board of Trustees of the University of the Arts Singapore. In her diplomatic career, she was Singapore's Ambassador to the United States and Singapore's Permanent Representative to the United Nations with concurrent accreditation as High Commissioner to Canada and Ambassador to Mexico.

Dr Carol Soon is a Senior Research Fellow at the Institute of Policy Studies where she heads the Society and Culture Department. Dr Soon is also Associate Director of the Asia Journalism Fellowship which is supported by Temasek Foundation. She is the Vice Chair of Singapore's Media Literacy Council and a member of the Industry Advisory Panel for the Humanities, Arts and Social Sciences at the Singapore University of Technology and Design. She serves on the Civil Service College-Ministry of Culture, Community and Youth Partnerships and Engagement Experts Panel. Dr Soon is a recipient of the Australian Endeavour Award and the Lee Kuan Yew School of Public Policy Research Excellence Award.

Dr Shashi Jayakumar is a Senior Fellow and Head of the Centre of Excellence for National Security at the S. Rajaratnam School of International Studies (RSIS). He was a member of the Singapore Administrative Service from 2002 to 2017. During this time, he was posted to various ministries, including the Ministries of Defence, Manpower, Information and the Arts, and Community Development, Youth and Sports. He was a Senior Visiting Research Fellow at the Lee Kuan Yew School of Public Policy from 2011 to 2014. Dr Jayakumar is also Singapore's representative (2022–2024) to the ASEAN Intergovernmental Commission on Human Rights.

ABOUT THE ILLUSTRATOR

Ang Qi Jun is an illustrator and designer. He likes to play video games in his free time. When he retires, he hopes to relax at a beach with his soft toys, Peanut and Curry, by his side.

Lecture I
THE SINGAPORE MEDIA'S LONG AND WINDING ROAD: 1824 TO 2022

LECTURE I

For today's lecture, I will be talking about the Singapore media. I will give a broad, historical view, to provide the context for the current media landscape. I should also explain: when I refer to "the Singapore media", I mean the legacy or traditional news media, including their digital versions, as opposed to the online-only media and social media. Also, the Singapore media is both print and broadcast. But I hope my broadcast colleagues will forgive me if I focus my views on the print media.

I should also clarify that I'm speaking in my personal capacity, although I am Interim CEO of the SPH Media Trust.

My lecture will be in three parts:

I start with the general issue of press freedom versus regulation of the media. I will speak on the key issues at the heart of today's press freedom debates, and link them to Singapore's current media laws, in particular the Newspaper and Printing Presses Act of 1974.

Next, I look back at the history of Singapore's English and vernacular media from 1824, when the first English paper was launched, focusing in particular on *The Straits Times* (*ST*) which was launched in 1845. I will also cover the Lee Kuan Yew government's crackdowns on the media after independence and its subsequent interventions to reshape the media landscape.

The third part of my lecture will cover the last two decades, in particular the digital disruption that hit the Singapore legacy media. I end by discussing the formation of the SPH Media Trust, which took over the media operations of Singapore Press Holdings (SPH) in December 2021.

Part I: Press Freedom vs Regulation

Let me start my lecture by discussing five issues that lie at the heart of the press freedom debates that are going on today.

1. *Freedom of Expression*

The constitutions of most democratic countries protect freedom of expression. But they can be divided into two groups. One group has freedom of expression with no caveats, and the other has freedom but with caveats.

Let us take a look at some constitutions in the first group which do not have caveats:

- The First Amendment of the United States (US) Constitution (1789):
Congress shall make no law respecting an establishment of religion, or prohibiting the free exercise thereof; or <u>abridging the freedom of speech, or of the press</u>; or the right of the people peaceably to assemble, and to petition the Government for a redress of grievance.[1]

- Article 19 of the United Nations (UN) Universal Declaration of Human Rights (1948):
Everyone has the right to freedom of opinion and expression; this right includes freedom to hold opinions without interference and to seek, receive and impart information and ideas through any media and regardless of frontiers.[2]

---

[1] Underline added.

[2] United Nations, "Universal Declaration of Human Rights," accessed April 14, 2022, https://www.un.org/en/about-us/universal-declaration-of-human-rights.

This is supplemented by Article 30:
Nothing in this Declaration may be interpreted as implying for any State, group or person any right to engage in any activity or to perform any act aimed at the destruction of any of the rights and freedoms set forth herein.

The constitutions with caveats include:

- Article 10 of the European Convention on Human Rights (1950):

Everyone has the right to freedom of expression. This right shall include freedom to hold opinions and to receive and impart information and ideas without interference by public authority and regardless of frontiers. This article shall not prevent States from requiring the licensing of broadcasting, television or cinema enterprises.

The exercise of these freedoms, since it carries with it duties and responsibilities, may be subject to such formalities, conditions, restrictions or penalties as are prescribed by law and are necessary in a democratic society, in the interests of national security, territorial integrity or public safety, for the prevention of disorder or crime, for the protection of health or morals, for the protection of the reputation or rights of others, for preventing the disclosure of information received in confidence, or for maintaining the authority and impartiality of the judiciary.[3]

- Article 11 of the Declaration of the Rights of Man (the French Constitution) (1789):

The free communication of ideas and opinions is one of the most precious of the rights of man. Every citizen may, accordingly, speak, write and print with freedom, but shall be responsible for such abuses of this freedom as shall be defined by law.[4]

Singapore is also in this latter category. Article 14 of the Singapore Constitution (1965) says this:

Freedom of speech, assembly and association
14. — (1) Subject to clauses (2) and (3) —

---

[3] European Court of Human Rights, Council of Europe, "European Convention on Human Rights," accessed April 14, 2022, https://www.echr.coe.int/documents/convention_eng.pdf.

[4] Government of France, "The Declaration of the Rights of Man and of the Citizen," accessed April 14, 2022, https://www.elysee.fr/en/french-presidency/the-declaration-of-the-rights-of-man-and-of-the-citizen.

> *(a) every citizen of Singapore has the right to freedom of speech and expression;*
>
> ...
>
> *(2) Parliament may by law impose —*
> *(a) on the rights conferred by clause (1)(a), such restrictions as it considers necessary or expedient in the interest of the security of Singapore or any part thereof, friendly relations with other countries, public order or morality and restrictions designed to protect the privileges of Parliament or to provide against contempt of court, defamation or incitement to any offence;*

It is clear that freedom of expression is absolute in America and the UN, but not absolute in other countries. This is where the problems begin. When Singapore sues a journalist here for defamation, it can be a breach of human rights in America.

But the Singapore Constitution is clear: there is no untrammelled freedom of expression.

2. *Freedom of the Press*

Only the US Constitution explicitly protects freedom of the press, again with no caveats. In most other countries, freedom of the press is not enshrined in the constitution but is an extension of freedom of expression. Most other countries, including Singapore, have no specific press freedom rights. The UN Charter also does not have specific freedom rights for the press.

As such, journalists outside of the US are protected only by their right to freedom of expression.

It should be noted that if you take "the press" to mean the platform provided by a proprietor to gather, process and disseminate information to a wider audience, then individual free speech and press freedom are not one and the same. Caveats and responsibilities, and regulations too, can be different for both. Here again, when a country has a media law, that law is seen as a breach of media freedom by some.

When I speak later about the World Press Freedom Index by the Paris-based Reporters Without Borders, I will argue that Singapore's media laws is the issue behind our low ranking. This is even though the European Convention on Human Rights allows for media laws.

3. *Media Laws*

Most countries have laws that restrict not only free speech but also press freedom. These include libel laws, sedition laws, privacy laws and press ownership laws. Interestingly, the US has ownership laws for television. Under these laws, Rupert Murdoch had to become a US citizen to own Fox Broadcasting Company.[5]

The rationale for media laws is that the press and broadcast players have tremendous power — both to advance the general good or to cause harm. The laws exist to make sure they do not cause harm.

A further rationale is that journalists and editors themselves need ethical guidelines so they do not abuse their power. The same goes for media owners who court political influence and are also driven by profit motives. The question is how to ensure these ethical guidelines are adhered to.

4. *The "Marketplace of Ideas"*

The notion of the "marketplace of ideas", popular in the US, needs defining. One definition I found is this: "The belief that the test of the truth or acceptance of ideas depends on their competition with one another, and not the opinion of a censor, whether government or some other authority".[6]

This draws on the economic marketplace analogy, where the best product wins in the market.

This idea is attributed to John Stuart Mill, regarded as the most influential English-speaking philosopher of the 19th century.[7] In his 1859

---

[5] Rupert Murdoch is the Executive Chairman of News Corp in Australia and the Co-Chairman of Fox Corp in the United States.

[6] David Schultz and David L. Hudson, "Marketplace of Ideas," *The First Amendment Encyclopaedia*, Middle Tennessee State University, 2017, https://www.mtsu.edu/first-amendment/article/999/marketplace-of-ideas.

[7] Christopher Macleod, "John Stuart Mill," in *The Stanford Encyclopaedia of Philosophy* (Summer 2020 Edition).

treatise *On Liberty*, Mill argued against censorship, saying the free flow of ideas is the best way to separate fact from falsehoods.[8]

Although the "marketplace of ideas" is not in any US law or statute, US courts have invoked this concept thousands of times to justify the First Amendment right to free speech. As one writer says, it "underpins much of First Amendment jurisprudence".[9]

5. *Media as the "Fourth Estate"*

The reference to the media as the "fourth estate" is now a faded idiom, but it is worth recounting how it arose after the French Revolution of 1789. The French call it *quatrième pouvoir* ("the fourth power") alongside the nobility, clergy and commoners.

The English prefer the word *estate* — which also has the meaning of a social or political class vested with distinct powers. To this day, the British Parliament comprises two of the estates — the House of Lords and the House of Commons. The other estate, the clergy, was disenfranchised centuries earlier.

What is the role of the press as the "fourth power"? Essentially, to check on abuse by those in authority, and to "speak truth to power".[10]

Thomas Carlyle, the Scottish historian and philosopher, attributed the term "fourth estate" to the British Member of Parliament, Edmund Burke, when he wrote: "Burke said there were Three Estates in Parliament; but, in the Reporters' Gallery yonder, there sat a Fourth Estate more important (by) far than they all."[11]

Carlyle also wrote in his history of the French Revolution: "A Fourth Estate, of Able Editors, springs up, increases and multiplies; irrepressible, incalculable."[12]

---

[8] John Stuart Mill, *On Liberty* (1859; reis., Canada: Batoche Books, 2001), 18–51.

[9] Schultz and Hudson, "Marketplace of Ideas."

[10] Simon Foley, *Understanding Media Propaganda in the 21st Century: Manufacturing Consent Revisited and Revised* (Cambridge: Cambridge Scholars Publishing, 2021), 7.

[11] Thomas Carlyle, *On Heroes, Hero-worship & the Heroic in History: Six Lectures* (London: J. Fraser, 1841), 265.

[12] Thomas Carlyle, "The Fourth Estate," in *The Works of Thomas Carlyle: The French Revolution: A History | Volume 2*, ed. Henry Duff Traill (Cambridge: Cambridge University Press, 2010), 235.

Press Issues in the Singapore Context

Let us next review these five issues in the Singapore context. First, where does the People's Action Party (PAP) government stand on these issues? I can list them out:

1. The government does not believe in the US' definition of free speech with no caveats. The caveats are written into the Singapore Constitution.
2. There is no provision for freedom of the press in the Singapore Constitution.
3. The government does not buy the idea of a "marketplace of ideas". It has said so, many times, from when Lee Kuan Yew was Prime Minister.
4. It does not agree with the Western-centric notion of the media as the "fourth estate" of the realm. Instead, the government wants the Singapore media to promote societal values and help in "nation-building".
5. The government believes in the need for media laws to guard against clandestine subversion of the media.

Here are some quotes from Lee Kuan Yew, who thought hardest about this and framed them as policy.

1. *Freedom of the press ... must be subordinated to the overriding needs of the integrity of Singapore, and to the primacy of purpose of an elected government.*[13]
2. *I said I did not accept that newspaper owners had the right to print whatever they liked. Unlike Singapore's ministers, they and their journalists were not elected.*[14]

Singapore's Media Laws

Let us look at how these views shaped Singapore's media laws.

---

[13] Lee Kuan Yew, "Address to the General Assembly of the International Press Institute at Helsinki, Wednesday, 9th June, 1971," accessed April 14, 2022, https://www.nas.gov.sg/archivesonline/data/pdfdoc/lky19710609a.pdf.

[14] Lee Kuan Yew, *From Third World to First* (New York: HarperCollins, 2000), 190.

The main law is the Newspaper and Printing Presses Act (NPPA) of 1974. This was a major piece of legislation that had a profound effect on newspaper companies. It has some unique provisions to regulate the ownership, management and financing of local newspapers.

The key features of the Act are as follows[15]:

- Ownership of newspapers is to be in Singaporean hands. All directors also have to be Singapore citizens.
- When passed in 1974, no single shareholder could own more than 5 per cent of the company. This was reduced to 3 per cent in 1977 and after a 2002 amendment, it has been raised to allow for a 12 per cent controller, including associates.
- Newspaper companies are required to create 1 per cent of their shares as management shares, to be held by parties approved by the Minister. A management share has 200 times the voting power of ordinary shares when it comes to the appointment of directors.
- Newspaper companies are prohibited from receiving funding from foreigners or foreign sources without government approval.
- The previous provisions for licences for printing presses, and yearly permits for newspapers, remain.
- In 1986, the Act was amended to allow the Minister to declare a foreign newspaper as "engaging in the domestic politics of Singapore" and to then restrict the number of copies it can distribute in Singapore.[16]

The result of the NPPA is that there can be no foreign ownership or influence in local publications, and no local newspaper barons either. This would prevent the role of a figure like Rupert Murdoch in Singapore.

The stated objects of the legislation were summarised well in Mary Turnbull's book, *Dateline Singapore: 150 Years of The Straits Times*. The objects were to[17]:

---

[15] Government of Singapore, "Newspaper and Printing Presses Act 1974," Singapore Statuses Online, accessed April 14, 2022, https://sso.agc.gov.sg/Act/NPPA1974?ProvIds=P11-#pr1-.

[16] Government of Singapore, "Newspaper and Printing Presses (Amendment) Act 1986," Singapore Statuses Online, accessed April 14, 2022, https://sso.agc.gov.sg/Acts-Supp/22-1986/Published/19860830?DocDate=19860830.

[17] Mary Turnbull, *Dateline Singapore: 150 Years of The Straits Times* (Singapore: Times Editions, 1995), 310.

- Ensure that newspapers were not used as instruments of subversion;
- Prevent the reproduction of foreign propaganda for subversion or undesirable purposes;
- Keep control of Singapore newspapers in the hands of Singapore citizens; and
- Avoid foreign manipulation.

It is hard not to draw the conclusion that the constant worry about subversion, which arose from the PAP's long fight with the communists, has shaped Singapore's media laws to this day.

Jek Yuen Thong, the Culture Minister then, said in his winding-up speech on the NPPA in 1974:

> ... it is not the intention of the government to go into the newspaper business. Our intention is to see that newspapers are properly managed and that they cannot be taken over by undesirable elements which may then direct their policies against the interests of our nation. That is the sole purpose of this Bill.[18]

Years earlier, in 1959, when Lee Kuan Yew and PAP did not get the support of *ST* in the inaugural Legislative Assembly General Election, he wrote a sharp letter to the paper, which was then still owned by British citizens:

> The folly of allowing newspapers to be owned by people who are not citizens or nationals of the country is that their sense of responsibility is blunted by the knowledge that if the worst came to the worst, they could always buzz off to some other place.[19]

Let me make a quick mention of other laws that affect the media sector.

First, the Broadcasting Act of 1994. The act regulates the operation and ownership of broadcasting services and allowed for reorganisation of the broadcast industry at the time. It also made changes to keep up with

---

[18] Singapore Parliamentary Debates, Official Report (27 March 1974) vol 33, (Jek Yeun Thong, Minister for Culture).
[19] Lee Kuan Yew, "Mr. Lee Kuan Yew Replies to the Straits Times," *The Straits Times*, May 22, 1959.

technological developments. The act also changed the definition of "broadcasting" to include programmes transmitted by whatever means.

The media also have to heed the Defamation Act (1957), Official Secrets Act (1935) and Internal Security Act (1960).

A recent new law is the Protection from Online Falsehoods and Manipulation Act (POFMA), introduced in 2019. This is aimed at tackling fake news and misinformation on digital platforms. It basically prohibits the communication of false statements of fact in Singapore.

In 2021, a new act called the Foreign Interference (Countermeasures) Act (FICA) was enacted. This gives the government the authority to investigate individuals suspected of being foreign agents engaged in hostile information campaigns.

The Singapore media's challenge is that it has to do its job within the ambit of these laws. I would point out that one feature of Singapore is that its laws are applied; they are not for show.

Thankfully, there is no regime of prior vetting of content in the news media by regulators. In the print industry, even SPH management does not vet content prior to publication.

What Do Singaporeans Think?

Where do Singaporeans stand on the issues I have covered thus far? I believe that it would be interesting to poll Singaporeans, especially the young generation. I hope that someone — perhaps the Institute of Policy Studies — will take this up.

The questions I would pose are the following:

1. Given the media laws, is there scope for the media to do a good professional job? Can it?

My view is, the media can, and it does. There are hundreds of good journalists in our media beavering away every day to produce good-quality, meaningful work, despite having to navigate the panoply of laws. Of course, it does mean having to "lawyer" some stories — the jargon for getting legal advice before publishing — just to make sure journalists do not get sued for defamation, for example. But this is no bad thing. If you have the power to defame someone, you need to have a care and a sense of fairness. Responsible editors and journalists not only double-check their facts before they publish but they also seek legal advice when necessary.

2. A second question: Is there room for a responsible watchdog role for the media?

I believe there is, but it cannot be the media's only role. You do not want a newsroom where journalists come to work and say: Who can I go after today? Equally, you do not want journalists to say: Which government policy can I promote today? What you want are journalists and editors who think hard about what stories our readers will want to read, or read more of.

3. Third, should the media play a societal or "nation-building" role?

The Singapore media is not averse to this, but again this need not be its sole role. During the COVID-19 pandemic, for example, there were many times when the media did play a responsible societal role. The media worked to correct misinformation and encouraged people to get vaccinated. They also played a part in explaining what the rules were, so people were not confused.

4. What about the notion of a "marketplace of ideas"?

My view is that if John Stuart Mill were living today, he would realise that the economic marketplace is one with plenty of fake goods. Finding the best product and avoiding scams is not easy. The marketplace of ideas is no different, especially in this day and age where misinformation is so rampant.

That said, one point I would make is, there is a growing desire among Singaporeans, both young and old, for a greater diversity of views. Of course, I am talking about genuine views — not views based on false facts, untruths and propaganda, and certainly not hate speech. This can be gleaned from one of the findings of a survey carried out by IPS after the last general election in 2020.[20]

5. What changes are needed to allow for a greater diversity of views?

Here again, for the media, the challenge is to take a middle road and strive for diversity and fairness. There is never a rock-solid consensus on any

---

[20] Carol Soon, "IPS Survey on Internet and Media Use during GE2020," October 8, 2020, https://lkyspp.nus.edu.sg/docs/default-source/ips/presentation-by-dr-carol-soon_ips-online-forum-on-internet-and-media-use-in-ge2020.pdf.

Figure 1.   Primary Reasons Behind People's Votes in Singapore's 2020 General Election

Primary reasons behind people's votes
"Which of the following was the primary reason behind your vote this election?"

Primary Reason for Voting	%
Quality of the candidates	21.4%
Having alternative views in Parliament	19.3%
Parties' track record	11.8%
I always vote for the same party	8.3%
Management of COVID-19	7.2%
Parties' positions on specific issues	5.2%
Parties' ideology in general	5.0%
Having a one-party majority in Parliament	3.8%
Dislike for one party beyond the reasons listed above	2.8%
Preference for one party beyond the reasons listed above	2.0%
Others	1.7%
Refuse to answer	11.6%

Source: Carol Soon, "IPS Survey on Internet and Media Use during GE2020," October 8, 2020, https://lkyspp.nus.edu.sg/docs/default-source/ips/presentation-by-dr-carol-soon_ips-online-forum-on-internet-and-media-use-in-ge2020.pdf.

policy. If you look at our election results, it would be safe to say that 30 to 40 per cent of voters have a different view of many things. The media has tried to reflect their views too.

One part of the media's job — telling the key facts first — is not well understood by many of the media's critics. Part of the problem is, this has become old-fashioned. Now, it is often a jumble of facts, interpretation and opinion. Some see this as "adding value" for readers. But the outcome is, if readers like your interpretation and opinions, they consider it a good story. If they do not, it is dismissed as a poor story. If you just give the facts, that is not good enough either. The problem is, it is becoming a more polarised world even here in Singapore.

Of course, which facts to select, and which to omit, is itself a challenge. But this is what professional journalists and editors do every day. It is also why critics see the Singapore media as "pro-government". They often say the media are just "regurgitating" the government's message. But they misunderstand the media's role. When you have a Committee of Privileges report that is a thousand pages thick, you want to present the key facts first and objectively. The commentary and opinion can be done separately, preferably on the same day too. Also, it is perfectly all right to leave readers to make up their minds once they have the facts.

This is not to say that the Singapore media gets this right all the time. Sure, they can improve, and I am sure they will.

On this, I should add that I am often challenged by the media as being pro-government. My response is that the Singapore media is pro *good* government. What if we had a bad and corrupt PAP government? My response is: That would be a different ballgame.

World Press Freedom Index (by Reporters Without Borders)

I must briefly address here a related subject — the World Press Freedom Index by Reporters Without Borders (also known as Reporters Sans Frontières, or RSF), the international non-government organisation whose aim is to safeguard media freedom and its right to freedom of information. Does Singapore really deserve its 160th place in the latest 2021 global ranking?[21] We are one above Somalia, one below Sudan and well below Russia and Myanmar too.

This ranking is baffling to many in the Singapore media as it is in total discord with reality. However, you must recall the five issues I outlined at the start.

I should first make clear this index evaluates the level of freedom available to the media in each country. It is not an indicator of the quality of journalism in the country. Unfortunately, some critics of the Singapore media do not seem to know the difference. Additionally, if indeed our press freedom regime is 160th, then it is amazing that Singapore journalists can produce work that win international awards every year. This fact seems to have eluded the RSF.

I do not have enough time to talk about RSF's opaque methodology. I will just make my main point: that RSF's main issue is with Singapore's media laws that I have spoken about.

---

[21] Reporters Without Borders, "Index Details: Data of Press Freedom Ranking 2021," accessed April 14, 2022, https://rsf.org/en/ranking_table.

When POFMA was passed in 2019, RSF described it as "an Orwellian law" and "a horrifying tool for censoring and intimidating online media outlets and Internet users".[22] The punishment was that our ranking fell seven places. When FICA was passed last year, RSF was even more apoplectic: "a legal monstrosity with totalitarian leanings".[23] It looks likely that Singapore will fall further in the next ranking. We will have to just shrug our shoulders and get on with our jobs.

Part II: Looking Back at The History
The Singapore Media in Colonial Times

Let me now move on to the second part of my talk, where I want to recap quickly the Singapore media's long and winding road, starting from colonial times. Not only does this story mirror Singapore's history but it also highlights the policy and other issues that I have discussed.

In 1824, when Singapore's first newspaper (the *Singapore Chronicle*) was launched, there was already a severe media licensing and vetting regime. This was established by the British East India Company, which was given the Queen's charter and trade monopoly east of the Cape of Good Hope.[24]

Apart from licensing, all materials had to be vetted prior to publication. Criticism of the company was forbidden, as was scandalous material about individuals. This regime came from the company headquarters in Calcutta, which applied its 1823 Act across all its territories including the Straits Settlements (Singapore, Malacca and Penang). Prior vetting of content was lifted only in 1833 and has never been reimposed since.

This raises an interesting question: Is there a difference between media regulation and censorship? Both involve supervision, control and at times suppression of information and ideas circulated within society. To me, the

---

[22] Reporters Without Borders, "RSF Explains Why Singapore's Anti-Fake News Bill is Terrible," April 8, 2019, https://rsf.org/en/news/rsf-explains-why-singapores-anti-fake-news-bill-terrible.

[23] Reporters Without Borders, "Singapore's Foreign Interference Bill — Legal Monstrosity with Totalitarian Leanings," September 23, 2021, https://rsf.org/en/news/singapores-foreign-interference-bill-legal-monstrosity-totalitarian-leanings.

[24] Turnbull, *Dateline Singapore*, 5–6.

key question is, what is the purpose? Is it to promote the public good? Or are there some other reasons? So yes, there is a difference, in my view.

In 1835, a second paper, *The Singapore Free Press*, was launched. Its backers were big names whose fame survive to this day: Edward Boustead, a prominent merchant; William Napier, Singapore's first lawyer and George Coleman, the leading architect and public works superintendent.[25] *ST* was Singapore's third English paper, founded in 1845 by an Armenian merchant, Catchick Moses, who appointed a British editor, Robert Carr Woods.

The 1840s was a period of high growth for Singapore. Its population grew from 40,000 to 60,000, and there was fierce competition between *ST* and the *Free Press*.[26]

In 1869, the Suez Canal was opened. There were weekly P&O sailings, and mail — including the news — took 40 days to arrive in Singapore from London.[27] In 1871, a sea cable was laid to Singapore, so cable news began.

Singapore also conducted its first proper census in 1871. The population consisted of "97,000 inhabitants, 922 Europeans and 2,200 Eurasians". The circulation of *ST* was at 300 in 1884.[28]

1914 saw the launch of the first locally owned and run English paper, the *Malaya Tribune*, founded by Dr Lim Boon Keng, a Singapore-born Peranakan physician who was also Singapore's first Queen's scholar. Funded by local Chinese businessmen and serving the local Asian population, it was called "the people's paper" and sold for 5 cents.[29]

In 1923, the Johor Causeway opened and *ST* began coverage of the Malay States. The paper even had its correspondent in Kuala Lumpur.

The 1930s saw intense media competition. In 1933, after a good run for almost a century, the *Free Press* was taken over by the Straits Times group. Notwithstanding this, the *Malaya Tribune's* circulation overtook *ST* to reach 13,000. In 1938, *ST* cut its cover price to 5 cents to match the

---

[25] Ibid.
[26] Ibid., 25.
[27] Ibid., 47.
[28] Ibid., 47–48, 52.
[29] Ibid., 70.

Malaya Tribune.[30] This bold move achieved its aim and *ST*'s circulation doubled to 15,000.

Mary Turnbull had this to say:

> *[The 1938 cover price cut] was probably the most important single decision ever taken in relation to the Straits Times because it changed the character of the paper, its aims and ambitions.*[31]

ST changed its content and included more coverage of "local events and Asian life". The paper also hired more English-educated Asian journalists, although senior posts were kept in the hands of expats.[32] This was when journalists like Wee Kim Wee, Chia Poteik, Harry Miller, Hugh Savage, Norman Seibel and TH Tan joined the *ST*.

During the World War II years, *ST* became the *Syonan Times*, and later the *Syonan Shimbun*.[33] After the war, *ST* resumed and chose to be a pan-Malayan national newspaper, printed in Singapore and sent to Kuala Lumpur.[34]

Interestingly, when *ST* became a public limited company in 1950, the paper's directors proposed the creation of 1 per cent management shares with 300 times the voting power, issued to the pre-listing owners so that they would remain in control. The use of management shares is also in today's NPPA.[35]

The Maria Hertogh riots of 1950 were another major turning point for *ST*. The riots arose after a custody battle over the 13-year-old daughter of a Dutch father and Eurasian mother who had been entrusted to a Malay family friend. The court decision to return the girl, brought up in a Muslim family, to her Christian birth parents resulted in three days of rioting, with 18 people killed and 173 wounded. Hundreds were arrested, and the press was blamed for igniting the riots.

---

[30] Ibid., 86–97.
[31] Ibid., 97.
[32] Ibid., 97–98.
[33] Ibid., 116–19.
[34] Ibid., 151.
[35] Ibid., 168–70.

Mary Turnbull wrote:

> *The Hertogh riots taught The Straits Times a sharp lesson, which was brought home all the more forcibly by the fact that Europeans and Eurasians were singled out for attack. ... The violence revealed deep racial passions below the deceptively calm surface, which could easily be unleashed by emotional reporting and dramatic pictures. ... From that time, the paper's policy was to tread warily and avoid inflaming racial or religious passions. The experience of the Hertogh riots proved a more effective and lasting lesson than restrictive legislation.*[36]

The next turning point for the media was the 1959 Legislative Assembly General Election, which saw Lee Kuan Yew contest to become Prime Minister of the first self-governing state. *ST* did not support Lee and the PAP, which resulted in furious attacks by Lee against *ST*.

When the PAP won the elections, *ST* moved its headquarters from Singapore to Kuala Lumpur. *ST*'s main newsroom, headed by Leslie Hoffman, a Singapore Eurasian, also relocated to Kuala Lumpur. Wee Kim Wee was then tasked to run the paper's Singapore branch operations.[37]

ST's headquarters returned to Singapore only in 1972 — some 12 years later and seven years after Singapore's separation from Malaysia. The main impetus was the Kuala Lumpur government's decision that its national paper could not be 70 per cent Singapore-owned. *ST* came back to Singapore and Malaysia started *The New Straits Times* in 1972.[38]

The Vernacular Press in Singapore
The Chinese-Language Media

Singapore's Chinese-language press has been in circulation for more than a century. They were launched by successful local Chinese businessmen

---

[36] Ibid., 175–78.

[37] Ibid., 214–19.

[38] Ibid., 294–98.

who were passionate about promoting Chinese culture and language. Being good businessmen, they also used their papers to promote their products.[39]

The earliest paper was *Lat Pau* which was started in 1881.[40] *Nanyang Siang Pau* was later established in 1923 by businessman and philanthropist Tan Kah Kee with the aim of promoting commerce and education. Tan used the printing press to print material for his rubber plantation business. The paper doubled up as an avenue to advertise his rubber products.[41]

Within a month of starting, the colonial government ordered the paper to stop publishing because of the pro-China stance of its contents. The newspaper resumed in 1924.

With the global economic recession then and the decline of the rubber industry, Tan's business faced a crisis and he sold the press to his son-in-law, Lee Kong Chian. After George Lee (Kong Chian's brother) died in 1965, his eldest son, Lee Eu Seng, took over as Managing Director and the company expanded.[42] The paper merged with *Sin Chew Jit Poh* to form *Lianhe Zaobao* and *Lianhe Wanbao* in 1983.

Sin Chew Jit Poh had been founded in 1929 by "Tiger Balm King" Aw Boon Haw. Aw started *Sin Chew* as an advertising channel for his Tiger Balm products. He had originally bought a tabloid newspaper, *Xing Bao*, which was later merged with Choon Guan Printing Press to publish *Sin Chew Jit Poh*.[43]

The masthead of *Sin Chew's* inaugural issue was written by Chiang Kai-shek, then president of the Republic of China. In his inaugural message, Chiang said the paper's duty was to attack anyone who went against his Kuomintang party. But his wider aim was to improve the position of overseas Chinese and promote Nanyang (i.e. Southeast Asian Chinese) studies.[44]

---

[39] Lee, *From Third World to First*, 185.

[40] Turnbull, *Dateline Singapore*, 51.

[41] Seow Peck Ngiam, "Nanyang Siang Pau," Singapore Infopedia, 2017, https://eresources.nlb.gov.sg/infopedia/articles/SIP_2017-01-10_095946.html.

[42] Ibid.

[43] Lee Mei Yu, "Sin Chew Jit Poh," Singapore Infopedia, 2020, https://eresources.nlb.gov.sg/infopedia/articles/SIP_2021-04-05_145051.html.

[44] Ibid.

Shin Min Daily News was started in 1967 by Singapore businessman Leung Yun Chee, the founder of Axe Oil, and Hong Kong writer Louis Cha, as an offshoot of Hong Kong's *Ming Pao*. The paper carried tabloid-style entertainment and local news with sensational headlines. Straits Times Press bought 45 per cent of *Shin Min* in 1982 and later bought it over completely.[45] It competed with *Lianhe Wanbao* in the evening paper market until the two papers merged in 2021.

Malay and Tamil Papers

The colonial era saw a plethora of Malay and Tamil papers. There were three papers in the Jawi script, with the first established in 1876. They were all helmed by Malay nationalists who wanted to uplift Singapore's Malay community. One Jawi paper, *Utusan Melayu*, founded by Yusof Ishak, who later became Singapore's first president, relocated to Kuala Lumpur in 1958 with a circulation of 35,000 a week. It continues today as *Utusan Malaysia*.[46]

There were even more Tamil newspapers, with the first published in 1875.

Only *Berita Harian*, founded in 1957, and *Tamil Murasu*, launched in 1935, have survived. Had they not been owned by SPH, they too might have closed.

Post-Independence: Government Involvement in the Singapore Media

I move now to the post-independence era to discuss the government's deep involvement in the Singapore media.

In Lee Kuan Yew's memoirs, *From Third World to First: The Singapore Story: 1965–2000*, he devoted a brief chapter titled "Managing the Media". Let me quote from his opening paragraph:

---

[45] Turnbull, *Dateline Singapore*, 347.

[46] Joshua Chia Yeong Jia and Nor-Afidah Abd Rahman, "Utusan Melayu," Singapore Infopedia, 2016, https://eresources.nlb.gov.sg/infopedia/articles/SIP_1088_2007-06-12.html.

> *In the 40 years since 1959, the Singapore press has evolved away from the norms set by the colonial government. We brought this about by laying down out-of-bounds markers, mostly for our English-language pressmen. They had been influenced by the British editors and reporters who used to be their superiors in the Straits Times group. It took many years before a younger generation of journalists in the 1980s recognised that the political culture of Singapore was and will stay different from the Western norm.*
>
> *However, our journalists are exposed to and influenced by the reporting styles and political attitudes of the American media, always sceptical and cynical of authority. The Chinese and Malay press do not model themselves on newspapers in the West. Their cultural practice is for constructive support of policies they agree with, and criticism in measured terms when they do not.*[47]

Since independence, government intervention in the media landscape came in two forms: (1) crackdowns against newspapers and editors and (2) interventions to reshape the media landscape.

Government Crackdowns Against the Media

The year 1971 was a tumultuous one for the Singapore media with a succession of crackdowns against the media.

The Eastern Sun

The Eastern Sun, an English-language daily run by Mr Aw Kow (of the Aw family that published *Sin Chew Jit Poh* and the former *Standard*), decided to close when the PAP government exposed that it had been funded by a communist news agency from China based in Hong Kong.[48]

---

[47] Lee, *From Third World to First*, 185.

[48] Turnbull, *Dateline Singapore: 150 Years The Straits Times*, 291.

The Singapore Herald

The *Singapore Herald*, an English newspaper, had its licence suspended. The government accused the paper of being involved in "black operations", being funded by foreign sources (including the Malaysian High Commissioner to Australia, Fuad Stephens), and spreading misinformation to stir feelings against Singapore's National Service policy.[49] The government also expelled three of its foreign editors.

Nanyang Siang Pau

In May 1971, in a move that rocked the media, four top executives of *Nanyang Siang Pau* were detained under the Internal Security Act. They included Lee Mau Seng, the former Managing Director and brother of Lee Eu Seng, editor-in-chief Shamsuddin Tung and two other senior staff. The following day, the paper ran an article titled "Our Protest", denying the allegations.[50]

Three weeks later, the government announced the four had confessed to "glamorising the communist system" and "working up communal emotions on issues over Chinese language and culture".[51] The paper ran a blank front page in protest the next day and held a press conference calling for an open trial.

The following month, all four issued affidavits denying their confessions. The four were promptly re-arrested and detained.

Lee Kuan Yew said in his memoirs: "… Nanyang Siang Pau turned rabidly pro-communist and pro-Chinese language and culture. We had to arrest Lee Mau Seng, the general manager."[52] Mau Seng was detained for two and a half years until his release on condition he emigrate to Canada as he had earlier planned to do.

---

[49] Tsun Hang Tey, "Confining the Freedom of the Press in Singapore: A "Pragmatic" Press for "Nation-Building"?" *Human Rights Quarterly* 30, no. 4 (2008): 876–905.

[50] Turnbull, *Dateline Singapore*, 291.

[51] Seow, "Nanyang Siang Pau."

[52] Lee, *From Third World to First*, 148.

In 1973, Lee Eu Seng, the elder brother of Mau Seng, was also arrested under the Internal Security Act for using the newspaper to "arouse and incite people against the Government over issues of Chinese language, education and culture".[53] He was detained for five years and released in 1978.

The upheavals of 1971–73 were the backdrop to the passing of the new Newspaper and Printing Presses Act in 1974.

Berita Harian

In 1976, in another crackdown by the Internal Security Department, the *Berita Harian (BH)* editor Hussein Jahidin and his deputy were arrested. At the same time, the Malaysian Special Branch arrested the top man in BH Malaysia, Samad Ismail, and his deputy. As Cheong Yip Seng wrote in his memoirs: "All four Singapore and Malaysian journalists were accused of using their newspaper to further the communist cause, with Samad as the puppet master."[54]

Both Samad and Hussein were former political detainees. Samad had been arrested and jailed twice by the British in the 1940s and 50s, and a young Lee Kuan Yew was his lawyer. According to Turnbull, it was Samad who opened Mr Lee's eyes to underground left-wing politics in Singapore.[55] After his release by the British, Samad became a founder member of the PAP but broke with Mr Lee who considered him an extremist. The Malaysian authorities detained Samad for five years until his release in 1981.

Lee Kuan Yew and The Straits Times: "The Knuckledusters Era"

It must have come as a relief to *ST* that it was not involved in the Internal Security Department's crackdowns. However, relations between Lee Kuan

---

[53] "Mr Lee Eu Seng Released from Detention," Ministry of Home Affairs Press Release, 1978, National Archives Singapore, accessed April 15, 2022, https://www.nas.gov.sg/archivesonline/data/pdfdoc/785-1978-02-01.pdf.

[54] Cheong Yip Seng, *OB Markers: My Straits Times Story* (Singapore: Straits Times Press, 2013), 147–48.

[55] Turnbull, *Dateline Singapore*, 210.

Yew and *ST* editors in the 1970s were still at a low. Cheong Yip Seng called it "the knuckledusters era" in his book.

Lee continued to be dismissive of journalists. For example, at a general election rally held in Fullerton Square in 1972, he said:

> *The not so bright go into political science and sociology. When they cannot get a good job, they go on to journalism. We are supposed to have freedom of the press. Their analysis of the PAP is often completely off mark. They do not know the basic data about men and politics in Singapore, that politics here literally mean life and death.*[56]

At another rally during the following general election, Lee warned:

> *If you read and you understand only the English language, then you are at a very grave disadvantage because you really don't know what is going on in a large part of Singapore. If you believe that the Straits Times and the New Nation is what Singapore is about, then you are living in a dream world.*[57]

One effect of Lee's hectoring was that *ST*'s management and board devoted much time discussing how to improve editorial quality. But progress was slow — at least to him.

One kerfuffle came when JB Jeyaratnam won the Anson by-election in October 1981. Lee blamed *ST*'s coverage and confirmed his view that it needed reorganisation if it could not put its own house in order.[58]

As Turnbull wrote:

> *The company feared that the government was planning an operation similar to the recent reorganisation of the transport system, when a government team of officials was sent in to*

---

[56] Lee Kuan Yew, as quoted in *Dateline Singapore*, 316.
[57] Ibid.
[58] Turnbull, *Dateline Singapore*, 334.

transform the inefficient bus companies into a profitable, effective system.[59]

It was this fear that led Peter Lim, then editor-in-chief of Straits Times Press, to propose to Lee Kuan Yew that S R Nathan be appointed Straits Times Press's executive chairman.

Nathan found morale low, but a further blow was to come, and he was just weeks into the job. Unbeknown to him, Lee was preparing for a major reshaping of the media landscape. The latter did not see this as an intervention but as stewardship of the media sector.

Formation of Singapore News and Publications Limited

In 1982, the government steered the merger of *Nanyang Siang Pau* and *Sin Chew Jit Poh* under a new holding company, Singapore News and Publications Limited (SNPL).[60]

The move came as a big shock, as the two papers and their owners were fierce rivals. The reason for the merger was to ensure the commercial viability of the Chinese press, in the face of the growing dominance of English and the lack of adequate talent to maintain high standards in many competing Chinese newspapers.[61]

This was not all. The government also gave an English newspaper licence to SNPL and a Chinese newspaper licence to Straits Times Press, which led to the publication of *Singapore Monitor* and *Shin Min Daily News*, respectively.[62]

The failure of *Singapore Monitor* — which closed in 1985 — drove home the cutthroat nature of media competition and why consolidating the local newspaper industry made sense.

---

[59] Ibid.
[60] Ibid., 342.
[61] Lee, "Sin Chew Jit Poh."
[62] Turnbull, *Dateline Singapore*, 342–47.

Formation of Singapore Press Holdings

There was more to follow. Two years later, in 1984, Straits Times Press, SNPL and Times Publishing Berhad announced that they would merge to form Singapore Press Holdings (SPH). It was clear that the formation of SPH was driven by Lee Kuan Yew, even though the government did not actively take part in commercial negotiations.[63]

The newspaper groups cited cutting costs from wasteful competition and duplication of resources as the main reasons for the merger.[64]

A key concern for the government was again the financial viability of the Chinese press as the move towards the use of the English language gathered speed.[65] Readership of Chinese papers was steadily declining. This trend coincided with the closure of Nanyang University, and a decrease in admissions to Chinese schools.

The government was conscious of the need to preserve space for the Chinese-speaking population and secure the institutions that sustained Chinese language and culture.[66] The period thus saw many related policy moves, such as the introduction of Special Assistance Plan (SAP) schools.

If the viability of the Chinese press was threatened, the threat that it would radicalise and agitate in the name of preserving Chinese language and culture would be far worse.

SPH and Mediacorp — Merger or Competition?

Another major attempt at reshaping Singapore's media landscape happened in the year 2000, which Cheong Yip Seng covered in detail in his memoirs.

---

[63] Cheong, *OB Markers*, 198.

[64] HistorySG, "Formation of Singapore Press Holdings," 2014, https://eresources.nlb.gov.sg/history/events/34789177-5f5e-468d-9a77-db3680ce4161.

[65] John A. Lent, "Restructuring of Mass Media in Malaysia and Singapore — Pounding in the Coffin Nails?" *Bulletin of Concerned Asian Scholars* 16, no. 4 (1984): 26–35.

[66] Turnbull, *Dateline Singapore*, 331.

The trigger was a corporate takeover in the US that shocked everyone in the global media industry. On 10 January, 2000, America Online, a young Internet company, announced it would acquire Time Warner, a long-established media giant, for roughly US$182 billion. This was an astonishing deal at the time and created a mega-corporation, AOL Time Warner, with dominant positions in everything from news, music, movies and entertainment to channels like cable and the Internet.

The merger came when dot-com companies were on a meteoric rise — it was only later called the "dot-com bubble" when they came crashing down. At the time, the new merged entity was considered the ultimate media empire.

The impact in Singapore was immediate, both in the media and the government. As Cheong wrote:

> *The old media business model was being overturned. No media conglomerate could survive the future without new media at its centre — that was the prevailing wisdom.*[67]

He went on to say:

> *This weighed on Lee Kuan Yew's mind. How would such American media giants as AOL Time Warner affect us? .... Lee Kuan Yew found the corporate consolidation argument compelling. If the Americans took this route, with the AOL Time Warner merger showing the way, could this be avoided here? Was there a case for an SPH takeover of Mediacorp, given that we (SPH) had more journalistic talent than the broadcaster?*[68]

I shall not recount the blow-by-blow details, but there was obviously pushback from Mediacorp and parts of the government. There were two camps — one arguing for a single combined media group, and another arguing for two competing multimedia groups.

---

[67] Cheong, *OB Markers*, 312.
[68] Ibid., 312–313.

"In the end," as Cheong wrote, "there was no consolidation. Instead, a full-blooded battle ensued between SPH and Mediacorp. We got our TV licence; they got a newspaper permit."[69]

Cheong also spoke about how, while all this was going on, a new radical publishing phenomenon had emerged — free newspapers, like the *Metro*, launched in Europe and were distributed in subways.[70]

Not surprisingly, Mediacorp chose this route. It hired PN Balji, then editor of SPH's *The New Paper*, to launch a free newspaper in Singapore. Meanwhile, SPH set up a TV company, Mediaworks, and hired Mediacorp's top TV executive, Lee Cheok Yew, to run it. SPH also stole a march and launched their own free sheet, called *Streats*.[71]

For the next four years, the two media groups were "locked in fierce combat on all fronts".[72] After losses of hundreds of millions of dollars, both sides agreed to a truce in 2004. SPH gave up its TV ambitions, closed down one of its stations and transferred the other to Mediacorp, and also stopped publishing *Streats*.[73]

For its part, Mediacorp sold a 20 per cent stake of its television business to SPH and 40 per cent of *Today*.[74] Cheong concluded, "The equity holdings meant little. They could not hide the cold reality that the media industry was back to square one."[75]

The final post-script came some years later. SPH unwound its Mediacorp equity holdings and *Today* gave up its print edition and is now a digital product. Over in the US, in 2009, Time Warner spun off AOL, ending that most ill-fated marriage.

---

[69] Ibid., 317.
[70] Ibid.
[71] Ibid., 318–319.
[72] Ibid., 320.
[73] Ibid., 327.
[74] Ibid.
[75] Ibid

Part III: The Last Two Decades

I come now to the final part of my talk: the last two decades. I will speak first about the digital disruption from around the year 2000 leading up to SPH Media's first-ever losses in 2020 and 2021.

I will then speak about the latest turn in our long road, the transfer of SPH Media from Singapore Press Holdings Ltd to the newly created not-for-profit SPH Media Trust.

I will also give my personal views on the debate in Parliament and the announcement of the S$180 million a year funding for SPH Media Trust (SMT) for five years in the first instance.

Disruption in the Media: Incumbent's Dilemma

In the 1990s, SPH was in the pink of financial health with reserves in excess of S$1 billion. I recall an annual general meeting where a shareholder asked Mr Lim Kim San, the executive chairman then: If there are no opportunities to invest the reserves, can you distribute some of it to shareholders? Why hold on to so much cash reserves?

I remember Mr Lim's answer. With a straight face, he said: "I like to have a full stomach." He assured the shareholder that SPH was actively looking for new opportunities and would keep shareholders posted.

One afternoon in 1996, when I was editor of *The Business Times*, our Executive Director, Tjong Yik Min, called me to his office. After some small talk, he asked me, "What would you say if I told you SPH was going to buy Paragon?" I replied: "The shopping centre? Why would we buy a shopping centre?" His reply surprised me: "Because the media business is a sunset industry." I pointed out that our media business was still making good margins. But he felt it was a matter of time before the impact of the Internet would be felt. The next day, SPH announced it was buying Paragon for S$682 million.

SPH's quandary all along has been that it is a living example of the "incumbent's dilemma". This is the flip side of the "innovator's dilemma". In our case, it was not as if we had our heads in the sand and did not see the coming disruptive technology — Yik Min saw that very early. SPH's problem was simply that disrupting and cannibalising a lucrative legacy business was easier said than done. In fact, it was just so hard.

All our print products launched digital editions very early in the mid-90s, but we were always keeping an eye on our legacy revenues. Many a time, editors had to hold our horses. As a listed entity, we would also have to justify to shareholders the need to make even bigger investments than we did.

As editor-in-chief, I used to get invites to talk about this at newspaper conferences. The theme was always digital disruption and the threats posed by the rise of Google, Facebook and the Internet media. (Instead of Meta, I will stick with calling it Facebook, if I may.)

There was one chart I used repeatedly to show how Google had no revenues in the year 2000, and how they found their path to profitability through digital advertising. Facebook followed soon after. Within 10 years, their revenues had overtaken the whole US newspaper industry's advertising revenues. This had not yet happened to SPH Media, but we knew it was a matter of time.

Let me show you that chart.

You will see that Google earned US$0.1 billion in 2001. By 2012, it was US$46 billion.

I used to tell my audiences: Google and Facebook are eating our lunch! These days, I am more charitable. They were not eating our lunch. Our customers had decided to have their lunch at Google and Facebook. And they did not come back.

This trend is also supported by tech platforms' recent advertising revenues. Google's 2021 advertising revenue figure is over US$209 billion.[76]

---

[76] Alphabet Inc., "Revenue Recognition," *Alphabet Annual Report 2021*, 60, accessed April 15, 2022, https://abc.xyz/investor/static/pdf/20220202_alphabet_10K.pdf.

Figure 2. Total US Newspaper Advertising Revenue vs Total Google Advertising Revenue (2001 to 2012)

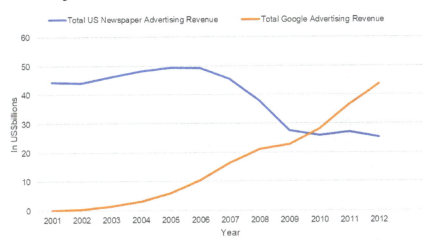

Source: Pew Research Center, Newspapers Fact Sheet, "Estimated Advertising and Circulation Revenue of the Newspaper Industry," June 29, 2021, https://www.pewresearch.org/journalism/fact-sheet/newspapers/; Statista, "Advertising Revenue of Google from 2001 to 2021," February 7, 2022, https://www.statista.com/statistics/266249/advertising-revenue-of-google/.

As for Facebook, it went from near-zero to US$115 billion in 2021.[77] These are huge numbers. They show how digital advertising is the money machine at the heart of the Internet.

SPH media, meanwhile, saw a secular decline in its advertising revenues from 2012. Unlike in other markets, we did not fall off a cliff. However, it has been a steady line downwards. SPH's response was to cut costs and downsize. Unfortunately, by 2020, together with the COVID-19 pandemic, our media business registered our first-ever loss.[78] The loss grew bigger in 2021. The challenge was to turn this around.

---

[77] Meta Platforms Inc., "Revenue," *Meta Annual Report 2021*, 93, accessed April 15, 2022, https://d18rn0p25nwr6d.cloudfront.net/CIK-0001326801/14039b47-2e2f-4054-9dc5-71bcc7cf01ce.pdf.

[78] Sue-Ann Tan, "SPH Posts First Net Loss of $83.7 Million Amid the Covid-19 Pandemic," *The Straits Times*, October 13, 2020, https://www.straitstimes.com/business/companies-markets/sph-posts-first-net-loss-of-837-million-amid-the-coronavirus-pandemic.

The saving grace is that Singapore's legacy media has not lost its audience. For SPH media, while its print readership fell, digital readers more than made up for it. And this is despite having paywalled sites.

Across all of the SPH platforms (print, digital, magazines and radio) and all languages, their reach is 73 per cent of all people aged 15 years and above in Singapore. For *ST* alone, the figure is 44 per cent.[79]

To illustrate our reach, I was copied on an email from Kishore Mahbubani after *ST* had run one of his columns where he told readers they could download a free digital copy of his latest book. Let me quote you what he said.

> Before the column appeared on Saturday, there had been about 140,000 downloads of the book. I expected *The Straits Times* article to generate 10,000 or at the most 20,000 additional downloads. Instead, to my absolute surprise, the number of downloads had increased to 223,000. In short, one article in *The Straits Times* generated 83,000 downloads. It was truly heartening to learn that my columns are being read and followed up on by such a large audience in Singapore.

One other metric to track closely is young readers. SPH media sites reach 44 per cent of those aged 15 to 24 years, and 46 per cent of those aged 25 to 39 years across all languages.[80] That is not bad for legacy media.

The success of leading sites like the *New York Times* has been an inspiration. They have shown there is a path to profitability through paid subscriptions. In fact, some of us spotted this ray of light some years ago, but SPH was not ready then to invest in an aggressive strategy. We now are.

---

[79] Singapore Press Holdings, "7 in 10 of Singapore Population Access SPH Content Properties Weekly, SPH Number 1 in Digital News: GfK Research," September 2, 2021, https://www.imsph.sg/7-in-10-of-singapore-population-access-sph-content-properties-weekly-sph-number-1-in-digital-news-gfk-research/.

[80] Grace Ho, "The Straits Times Remains Best-Read title, With Clear Shift to Digital, Across All Age Groups: Survey," *The Straits Times*, September 20, 2021, https://www.straitstimes.com/singapore/community/the-straits-times-remains-best-read-title-with-clear-shift-to-digital-across-all.

I am glad that from the start, SPH decided not to give away our digital content for free and experimented with paywalls. They took a lot of flak for this but stuck with it. SPH Media now has more than 400,000 paying subscribers. This is a good base to grow from.

Much of SPH digital content is in fact free, with only premium content behind the paywall. Throughout the ongoing pandemic, almost all its COVID-19 coverage has been free.

Going forward, one area to watch is how regulators in the US and European Union review their Internet regulations to combat the deluge of misinformation, propaganda and outright fake news. Will Section 230 of the US Communications Decency Act of 1996, dubbed "the 26 words that created the Internet", be amended to restore a greater degree of trust?[81]

Section 230 of the US Act says this: "No provider or user of an interactive computer service shall be treated as the publisher or speaker of any information provided by another information content provider."

Fortunately for us, trust in Singapore's legacy media is high. Minister Josephine Teo highlighted this in her speech in February 2022.[82]

To sum up, legacy media have the readership, the paid subscriptions (which means its products are of value) and the trust. Now it needs to find the path to growth and profitability.

SPH Media Trust: A New Model

This brings me to the present, and the SPH Media Trust.

I will just get straight to the news from Parliament that the SPH Media Trust will receive annual funding of up to S$180 million for five years.[83]

---

[81] Jeff Kosseff, *The Twenty-Six Words That Created the Internet* (New York: Cornell University Press, 2019), 3.

[82] Josephine Teo, "MCI response to PQ on Update on Discussion with SPH Media Trust on Funding Support and Measures to Ensure Its Sustainability in Highly Competitive Media Industry and Limited Local Market," Transcript of speech delivered at Parliament Sitting on February 15, 2022, https://www.mci.gov.sg/pressroom/news-and-stories/pressroom/2022/2/mci-response-to-pq-on-update-on-discussion-with-sph-media-trust-on-funding-support-and-measures-to-ensure-its-sustainability-in-highly-competitive-media-industry-and-limited-local-market.

[83] Ibid.

The SPH Media Trust will surely use the grant prudently and account for its use. It will invest in technology and capabilities to expand digital outreach and improve customer experience. At the same time, it will continue to seek commercial revenues and new revenue sources.

The Ministry of Communications and Information's funding comes with a heavy responsibility. Everyone in the SPH Media Trust, from top to bottom, and across the four languages, will have to demonstrate that they are worthy of this funding.

And because government funding is the acknowledgement of what the SPH Media Trust has been saying — that being a trusted and credible media *is* a public good — this cannot just be a slogan. The SPH Media Trust will have to live it, guard it and not betray it. Everyone in the organisation has to be driven by this purpose.

The SPH Media Trust newsrooms will no doubt welcome the assurance of editorial independence. The key quote for me was when Minister Josephine Teo said: "No one gains if these products lack credibility and are ignored by audiences. On the contrary, we are funding them precisely because they do have readers who trust them."[84]

But I expect there will be plenty of issues, especially from media critics, over editorial independence. Already, Leader of the Opposition Pritam Singh has asked how Singaporeans would be assured that SPH Media Trust's content would not be "tainted by allegations" of political interference.[85] The problem is, to taint with allegations is easy to do but to prove or disprove them is harder. This is why I have all along taken the line that the proof will be in the pudding, in particular the judgment of readers at large, both at home and abroad.

One objective all of us share is an informed and engaged citizenry. Here, how the media deals with issues of diversity of views and fairness

---

[84] Ibid.

[85] Justin Ong, "SPH Media Trust Has Exercised Editorial Independence, This Will Not Change with Govt Funding: Josephine Teo," *The Straits Times*, February 15, 2022, https://www.straitstimes.com/singapore/politics/sph-media-trust-has-exercised-editorial-independence-this-will-not-change-with-government-funding-josephine-teo.

(that I spoke about earlier) will matter. Ways must be found to handle misinformation, propaganda, plain falsehoods and hate speech, and also help prevent polarisation. All of this is work to be done.

A final thought. This is a new model — a commercial/public not-for-profit model — which may take some time to work through. Some of us had made hopeful predictions about new models, because we could see that the purely commercial model, and especially a listed company model, was not likely to lead to good outcomes.

Let me end by saying we are now on the latest new stretch of the Singapore media's long and winding road. I hope the next media person who will speak on this subject will have good results to share.

Question-and-Answer Session
Moderated by Professor Chan Heng Chee

Mr Patrick Daniel speaking with Professor Chan Heng Chee at the Q&A session
Source: Jacky Ho for the Institute of Policy Studies

Professor Chan Heng Chee: Thank you very much for the riveting and comprehensive tour d'horizon of the Singapore media landscape, and more accurately, the print landscape. I think you underestimated how long the winding road would take! But you have tackled all the key issues and highlighted Singapore's attempts, or more accurately Mr Lee Kuan Yew's attempts, to shape a media model that works for Singapore — one that serves Singapore and its needs.

People talk of models for the press. There are three models that have come about, and you have described some. First, there is the liberal democracy press model, and even in a liberal democracy, there are degrees of freedom of press, which you have demonstrated. So it is more accurate to talk of models of press in liberal democracy. For example, in the US, there are no caveats, whereas in other countries, there are caveats, press councils and so on. Second, you also have the totalitarian communist authoritarian press.

As a political scientist and as someone interested in development, I read a lot about the development press in the 1960s. I think you were trying to describe development journalism in your lecture. In a way, Singapore was searching for that sort of model. There are two ways of looking at the development press or development journalism. One is development done by the experts — the engineers who want to bring development to communities and want to communicate to people the goals of this development. The other is a straight development press, which is when the press is used to support the country in nation-building.

In the 1960s, a lot of new states were emerging and I think Lee Kuan Yew might have been reaching out for a development press model and development journalism. As we know in press theory, there is theory and there is practice. Even in the liberal democracy press model, you have theory and practice. Among the liberal democracies that we have seen, are all these presses truly liberal? Who owns them? Who controls them? Ownership dictates many things. People can buy a press and make it an advocacy tool for a particular point of view or a particular ideology. All this is becoming clearer today. So, even in a liberal democracy press, the practice may be slightly different and Mr Murdoch has been pushing his point of view very successfully. In fact, in Australia, Kevin Rudd and Malcolm Turnbull, two former prime ministers, ran a petition to try to get a commission established to see whether the Murdoch press was controlling too much of the Australian press and pushing a point of view. We can see the problems there.

My question for you is this. Certainly, and especially in the early days of our independence, we were looking for a press that supports the government in nation-building and in producing the right policies for the right society. However, you said there is room now in the media for diversity and that people want diverse views. How would you achieve that diversity?

Mr Patrick Daniel: Yes, that is the question that I am posing too.

Prof Chan: I am saying all this taking fake news into consideration.

Mr Daniel: We can put that aside and assume we can deal with fake news, propaganda and so on. Among reasonable people and with reasonably coherent arguments, you can make two very different arguments on anything, whether it is minimum wages or economic policy. I think that we need, going forward, to engage with more groups of people and have more debates.

Prof Chan: Will you publish them?

Mr Daniel: Of course! Why do people think we do not publish them? Of course, we do.

I would want to find out why people think they will not be published. It could be that it has less to do with the government than the fact that we have a group of writers we work with regularly. Perhaps we ought to go out and look for different views and invite them to write for us. I feel we should get the facts on this — get someone independent to do a poll and then move in the direction of the results. I hear what you are saying, and if indeed it is because we do not publish alternative views, then we have to reflect and say we cannot continue like this. I do not think that is the case, though. We have control over our op-ed pages, and for our op-ed pages, we are talking about a different group of readers. We are not trying to influence people in the local news pages. So, I think there is room and we must do it.

Prof Chan: You have answered one question I was going to ask you, but I will still put it to you. *The Straits Times* is seen to be the voice of the government. You have explained that you do not apologise for that and indeed, I also see some role that the press should be playing in explaining government policy well. However, the question is whether you would have op-ed pieces that differ from the policy? Would *The Straits Times* run them? I do see a bit of this kind of debate in foreign policy. You can publish a foreign policy op-ed that differs from the foreign policy we are pursuing. But in domestic policy, this does not happen as often. So would *The Straits Times* publish that?

Mr Daniel: I cannot speak on behalf of the current team in *The Straits Times*, but I would like to think that for sure, they should have more voices. But I would say that some of these descriptions of *The Straits Times* actually carry over from the 1990s — people form their opinions and they have not changed their views. Actually, I get criticised by opposition party members all the time. But the reason people know of the opposition members is because they are carried in the legacy media. Look at opposition members like Pritam Singh and Sylvia Lim, and the amount of space they get in our newspapers. Where do you think people find out about them? That is why I personally think it is a little bit unfair. I think there is a lot of space given to them. I do not see why, if we are doing it for the news pages, we cannot do that in the op-ed pages as well.

So, I hear you and I think that is the reason why we must poll people and see whether their views are up to date or not. But I think we get a bit of a bad reputation from our legacy, because we are the legacy media. So if we had issues before, it just takes a long time for readers to change their views. But you raised a good point because we have to make a decisive move so that people know that we have changed and then maybe their views might change.

Prof Chan: Let me follow up with another question. You have been in the press for 30 years now. Have you had a period where you felt that there was more space and room for the papers to print what they wanted? That the space had expanded? And the converse of that, were there times when the space contracted? And if you felt that. What did these changes correspond with? Was there an external event or were there domestic events that changed the circumstances and caused the loosening or tightening to happen?

Mr Daniel: My immediate response to that is that it depends on who the Prime Minister is. For sure when Lee Kuan Yew was the Prime Minister, he was a real activist and he was really vested with the media, in the sense that he knew the power of the media and engaged them. In fact, among all the three prime ministers, he was the one who put aside the most time to talk to us and ask us what we thought. He gave us a lot of time and a lot of engagement. Of course, he was trying to persuade us to his point of view but he did make an effort to tell us why he was doing what he was doing. When we had lunches with him, I found that he appreciated it when I just told him exactly what I thought. He would scold me at times, but I knew it registered in his head. There were times when I would tell him something he did not know but he would always check on what I told him, so I could not just spin inaccuracies. So, although he would track what we wrote about, he engaged us as well.

It got easier with Goh Chok Tong. We had a good relationship with him. With Lee Hsien Loong, there are no issues. He understands the media well and he does not need to try and shape our views, so it has gotten better. I told you all the things that Mr Lee Kuan Yew had to say about "knuckledusters" during my lecture. All that is history. I think there is now a lot more space for the media to do things so I am surprised you asked if we would run certain pieces. When I was the editor and you wrote a good piece that disagreed with policy, I would run it. I am sure my colleagues will do the same.

Prof Chan: I have a few questions here. You talk about the inaccuracy of the World Press Freedom Index. In your opinion, how should press freedom be more accurately measured?

Mr Daniel: Reporters Without Borders have somewhat monopolised this index. There are few other similar indices. I did not go into it in my lecture, but I would like to look at their methodology to see whether it is accurate. I looked for their criteria — it is hard to find — but when I did, something struck me. They have six criteria, and a seventh criterion too, which is the number of journalists who are killed or arrested. Then they calculate two indices — one with the seventh criterion and one without it. For journalists murdered, Singapore got top marks.

Prof Chan: Because journalists were not murdered, just to be clear.

Mr Daniel: Sorry yes, for not being murdered. What they do is they take the worse of the two indices, to prevent an inappropriately high ranking from being given to a country where few or no acts of violence against journalists take place, although the provision of news is tightly controlled, according to Reporters Without Borders.[86] What kind of index is this? It measures two indices, and Singapore is number 160 because you do not consider that criterion on murders. So, I have my doubts about the methodology.

Prof Chan: Should our press engage with the people who created this index?

Mr Daniel: I have been editor-in-chief for many years and not once did they want to engage. Not that I looked for them, but if they came and asked to talk about press freedom, I would have been happy to speak to them. But there is opacity in the methodology. I do not want to rubbish them, because they have been doing it for a long time, but I would press for an audit of that methodology.

Prof Chan: Now, there is a question on the Media Trust. How does SPH Media Trust assure us of editorial independence when it gets its money from the government? This is especially important, with powerful laws like the Newspaper and Printing Presses Act in play as well. Besides producing a good product, do you think changes are needed in the laws to relax the

---

[86] Reporters Without Borders, "Detailed Methodology," accessed September 1, 2022, https://rsf.org/en/index-methodologie-2013-21.

government's hold on the editors and management to give more leeway for editorial independence?

Mr Daniel: We put out newspapers every day. We cannot run and we cannot hide. You read our papers and you know whether we are balanced and fair and whether we are giving alternative views and the full picture. If we see a very biased article, you and I can spot it instantly. So, this idea of independence might be something in people's heads. They think that the government is telling us what to write. I am saying to you the judgement can be made very easily — just read the paper and you can tell whether it is one-sided or not. I am confident that going forward, we will be able to show that we produce good, balanced articles that readers will be informed by or better still, educated by. The challenge is, how can I assure them of this? I do not quite know how to do it. What is it that you want me to demonstrate? What would satisfy you? It is tough. My colleagues and I will just do our best and if the judgment is that this is a terrible paper, we will know very quickly that we are doing a bad job.

Prof Chan: This next question, from the audience, is straightforward. Will *The Straits Times* publish a parliamentary speech by an opposition politician as it does for government officials?

Mr Daniel: We have! Of course, we have.

Prof Chan: I think I have read some.

Mr Daniel: Can we do more? Yes. But they must be worth publishing, not that they are not. I am saying we have and we will. Actually, do you know who complains the most about articles never being published? Members of Parliament from the People's Action Party.

Prof Chan: There are many of them.

Mr Daniel: Yes, there are so many of them. We get lots of material. We get complaints from both sides, so we must be doing something right. But I can tell you we have published parliamentary speeches by opposition politicians.

Prof Chan: We still have some time. Is the subscription model really viable for legacy media outlets like *The Straits Times* especially when so many news outlets provide stories for free?

Mr Daniel: Good question. We have thought very hard about this from the start. We do have about 400,000 paying subscribers so we are making progress. There are three main paying papers: *The Straits Times*, *Zaobao* and *Business Times*. *Berita Harian* is also charging but they have small numbers. We are going along that road but we have not pushed very hard. We do not sell overseas and we do not sell to corporates. There are good examples of newspapers that have succeeded in using the subscription model. Of course, these are big names like *New York Times* and we are not there yet in terms of our coverage. But we want to aspire in that direction. Now, can we give our content for free? Yes, we can, but I think the test of whether a paper has value is if people are prepared to pay for it.

Prof Chan: Actually, I noticed that a lot of newspapers that used to give content for free are now charging and offering subscriptions.

Mr Daniel: Correct. That was the second point I wanted to make, which is that people are accepting this. And papers are realising that if they fight for readership in the free space, there is even more competition. That is why many papers are moving in the direction of serving their readers well and charging for their content. I am glad that SPH started charging very early under all our CEOs. Of course, we experimented with different kinds of paywalls. We now put much of our content before the paywall, which is free, and the premium content behind the paywall. All our COVID-19 content, for instance, is free.

Prof Chan: And I would like to make the point and a plea to readers that if we want quality journalism, we should pay for it. Because the organisation has to survive and journalists have to be paid. We want good stories, so we should support them with the means and resources for journalists to go after their stories.

There is another question: How do you encourage and provide the space for deeper, more thoughtful articles on topics like solidarity and identity which you can publish? I think the academics try to write for you, sure, but not enough on identity, justice or solidarity.

Mr Daniel: There is an inherent bias in the media to go after the "newsy" items. For example, what is happening in Ukraine and the war with Russia. Even the academics are writing more on these areas, as well as topics like China and US relations. So if we get a piece on solidarity, it would have to be very good — super-duper, in fact — to claim space in our papers. But it is a fair point. I think we should not be dominated by news and "newsiness" even in our commentary pages.

Prof Chan: I hardly have time left but I want to read you this question: If you were in Mr Lee's shoes, would you have approached media governance differently? Would you have taken a more contest-of-ideas approach for instance?

Mr Daniel: Mr Lee Kuan Yew did things the way he did because he was a real fighter. He was very passionate about many things, such as the media. He was an activist and he wanted to get things done. I am not him. You have got to be really tough and really strong to say, "This is the right way to go," even on issues that have nothing to do with you. And to say this not only to government agencies but to private media companies as well. Goh Chok Tong never did that and Lee Hsien Loong was not like that. If Lee Hsien Loong had a major issue, he might call the chairman and tell him what he thought and then he would leave it with the board and editors. I would approach it that way too, like a good corporate person.

Prof Chan: We have one last question. Besides the Singapore audience, will SPH try to expand its reach overseas? What is its priority? The local market or the wider audience?

Mr Daniel: We are definitely going overseas, but we want to keep our local audience too — there is no doubt about that. It is not an either/or. We want to grow locally. We have good reach locally, but we have to make sure that, through encouraging diversity, for instance, we keep the local market. However, we have not done enough to go overseas. We will, for sure, and I think we will succeed, because I do think we have a product that can travel.

Prof Chan: Well thank you very much, Patrick. I found this fascinating. It was long but worthwhile. It has been a pleasure to be in conversation with you here and to listen to you. I am sure the audience enjoyed this presentation as well. Thank you very much for being with us this afternoon.

Lecture II
GRAPPLING WITH THE DARKER SIDE OF THE INTERNET: A GLOBAL CHALLENGE

LECTURE II

The topic of my second lecture today is on the Internet, in particular the global challenge of regulating the Internet's darker side. The first part will be on the phenomenal beneficial impact the Internet has had, partly the result of its open-access architecture and light-touch governance. The second part will focus on the darker side of the Internet, and I will use digital advertising as a case study. My concluding part will focus on the way forward for Internet governance.

I should first make my usual declaration that I am again speaking in my personal capacity. I should also declare my interest as a longtime member of the legacy media and Director of the SPH Media Trust.

In my first lecture, I covered the severe digital disruption that the legacy media has faced as a result of the rise of big tech platforms. My second lecture is about the Internet, which necessarily covers the big tech players. But I am putting aside today the competitive issues between the legacy media and new media. I am stepping back to focus on the broader issue of Internet governance, which I believe is an urgent public policy issue that affects all of us. I genuinely believe that unless the global governance model is reviewed, trust in the entire Internet ecosystem will inevitably be seriously eroded. The bigger danger is that any fallout will harm the wider financial and economic system.

Part I: The Phenomenal Impact of the Internet
My Introductory Story

By way of introduction to my topic, I have a brief story to tell. In November of 2016, my wife and I were on a driving holiday in the United States (US) when their presidential election was in full swing. This was the election involving candidates Donald Trump and Hillary Clinton. On election day of 8 November, I drove from Chicago to a place called Door County on the shores of Lake Michigan. It was pretty much in the middle of nowhere. I stopped to fill some petrol and then chatted with the cashier, a middle-aged lady.

"Have you gone out to vote?" I asked her. "Yes," she said. And without any prompting, she told me she had voted for Trump. Then she added: "I can't bear that evil paedophile." When I looked at her somewhat blankly, she said: "Haven't you heard? Hillary Clinton is running a child sex ring in Washington, D.C." It was in fact the first time I was hearing it, but I said to her: "Surely you don't believe that story." "You bet I do!" she shot back. "It's all over the Internet." I smiled, took my change and left.

When we reached our motel, I did a Google search. Sure enough, the story of Hillary and her Satanic paedophile ring operating out of a pizza restaurant in Washington, D.C. was all over social media. But it was an obvious piece of fake news, or what I call wilful misinformation.

I recount this story to show what I mean by the darker side of the Internet. Just this one piece of wilful misinformation that went viral — it was tweeted 1.4 million times — might well have lost Hillary Clinton the election and made Donald Trump President.[1] I remember watching Jake Tapper on CNN that evening as the election results came in. He was at a complete loss as to how the entire polling profession got it so wrong. I think the Internet's darker side played a big part in that election result and may have shifted the course of history.

But I am running ahead of myself. I will come back to this subject a little later. Let me first recap the rise of the Internet and the phenomenal impact it has had.

Milestones in the Rise of the Internet

The Internet has changed everyday life for literally billions of people and taken human communication to an altogether new level. In that sense, it is the most far-reaching invention the world has seen. It has brought a whirlwind of benefits like no other.

Previous centuries have of course seen transformative advances. In particular, I refer to the first two industrial revolutions in the 18th and 19th centuries, driven first by steam engines and then electric power. The Internet is a child of the third industrial revolution, also called the digital revolution as it is marked by the pervasive shift to digital electronics, in particular digital computing and communication technologies.[2]

Figure 1 shows a chart of the milestones in the early development of the Internet.

I should explain at this point the terms "Internet" and "World Wide Web", which are often used interchangeably. Strictly speaking, they are different. The Internet is the infrastructure that connects *devices* in the

---

[1] Amanda Robb, "Anatomy of a Fake News Scandal," *Rolling Stone*, November 30, 2017, https://www.rollingstone.com/feature/anatomy-of-a-fake-news-scandal-125877/.

[2] "The Third Industrial Revolution," *The Economist*, April 21, 2012, https://www.economist.com/leaders/2012/04/21/the-third-industrial-revolution.

Figure 1. Milestones in the Rise of the Internet

Source: Information compiled from: "Timeline of Computer History," Computer History Museum, accessed August 25, 2022, https://www.computerhistory.org/timeline; Defense Advanced research Projects Agency (DARPA), accessed August 25, 2022, https://www.darpa.mil/attachments/DARAPA60_publication-no-ads.pdf, 4; "Key milestones in the development of Internet", *The Sydney Morning Herald*, August 31, 2009, https://www.smh.com.au/technology/key-milestones-in-the-development-of-internet-20090831-f43x.html.

network. The World Wide Web is the way *information* is shared via the Internet.[3]

For simplicity, when I refer to the Internet in my lecture, I include the World Wide Web, or the Web for short. When I do refer to the Web, I will be referring specifically to the information-sharing aspect of the Internet.

The Internet thus has two parts:

(1) a global networking infrastructure that allows instant connectivity between devices; and
(2) a system for instant access and sharing of information.

---

[3] "World Wide Web vs Internet — What's the Difference?" *BBC*, March 11, 2019, https://www.bbc.co.uk/newsround/47523993#:~:text=The%20world%20wide%20web%2C%20or,connect%20towns%20and%20cities%20together.

But the Internet has achieved much more than just connectivity and information sharing. It has sparked an explosion of creativity and innovations, including the integration of many technology capabilities in unprecedented ways. This is the reason it has become such a popular and far-reaching phenomenon.

Since 1983, when the Internet started, and especially after 1990, when the Web kicked in, the number of global Internet users has exploded off the chart. The latest number of global Internet users in 2021 was 4.9 billion — or 60 per cent of the world's total population.[4]

Not surprisingly, right from its start, the Internet and the Web created a boom in new opportunities for businesses, and for investors too. In the 1990s, many Internet-related companies, dubbed "dot-coms", rushed to be listed on stock markets and saw their stock prices soar, making their young founders instant millionaires. This started the dot-com boom of the late 1990s, which later proved to be a bubble.

A major milestone of that era was the stunning takeover of Time-Warner by America Online (AOL) in January 2000 for roughly US$182 billion, an astronomical sum back then. It was a dazzling start to the new millennium which I spoke of in my first lecture.

Between 1995 and 2000, the technology-dominated Nasdaq index rose from under 1,000 to more than 5,000. But it came crashing down in 2001 and many dot-coms went bust. This was essentially an Internet-generated global financial crash.[5]

But the strongest Internet companies survived, reviewed their practices and prepared to compete in a new economy which was dubbed Web 2.0. A second wave of Internet companies arose, led by the likes of Google,

---

[4] International Telecommunication Union, "Individuals Using the Internet," [2005–2021 data], accessed April 22, 2022, https://www.itu.int/en/ITU-D/Statistics/Pages/stat/default.aspx.

[5] Walter Hamilton, "Nasdaq's Stunning Rise Carried Index Past 5,000," *Los Angeles Times*, March 10, 2000, https://www.latimes.com/archives/la-xpm-2000-mar-10-mn-7290-story.html.

Amazon, eBay and Facebook. One feature of that period, especially in the mid-2000s, was the rush of mergers and acquisitions. In 2005 and 2006, Google purchased YouTube for US$1.65 billion, eBay bought Skype for US$2.6 billion and News Corp bought Myspace for US$580 million.[6] During those two years alone, the Internet economy grew more than it had during the entire dot-com boom.

Looking back, the amazing thing about the Internet phenomenon is that it happened in the span of just a few decades — four decades if you take 1983 as the start, and two decades if you take the post-dotcom period. We are all fortunate to be living witnesses of this digital revolution and the dawn of the Information Age. It is a revolution that shows no sign of slowing down. In fact, it looks to be speeding up even more and we will have to hang on to our seats. Remember, we are just in the 23rd year of a new century and a whole new millennium.

In fact, some writers are already saying we are entering the Fourth Industrial Revolution. What is this next revolution? One definition I came across put it this way: "It is characterised by a fusion of technologies that is blurring the lines between the physical, digital and biological spheres."[7] I do not know about the biological aspect, but the blurring of the physical and the digital is enough to boggle us all. I will speak on this in my third and final lecture.

For now, I want to highlight the phenomenal impact the Internet has had. It has been projected that almost four out of five people in the world

---

[6] "Google buys YouTube for $1.65 billion," *NBC News*, October 9, 2006, https://www.nbcnews.com/id/wbna15196982; Ken Belson, "EBay to Buy Skype, Internet Phone Service for $2.6 billion," *The New York Times*, September 13, 2005, https://www.nytimes.com/2005/09/13/technology/ebay-to-buy-skype-internet-phone-service-for-26-billion.html; Jennifer Saba, "News Corp Sells Myspace, Ending Six-Year Saga," *Reuters*, June 30, 2011, https://www.reuters.com/article/us-newscorp-myspace-idUSTRE75S6D720110629.

[7] Klaus Schwab, "The Fourth Industrial Revolution: What It Means, How to Respond," *World Economic Forum*, January 14, 2016, https://www.weforum.org/agenda/2016/01/the-fourth-industrial-revolution-what-it-means-and-how-to-respond.

Figure 2. Monthly Active Users of Selected Social Media Platforms as of January 2022

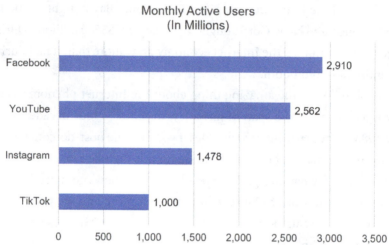

Source: Adapted from Simon Kemp and DataReportal, "Digital 2022: Global Overview Report," January 26, 2022, https://datareportal.com/reports/digital-2022-global-overview-report, 99.

will be Internet users by 2030.[8] Social media platforms are also reporting massive user numbers. As of January 2022, Facebook had 2.9 billion monthly users and YouTube had 2.6 billion.[9] Internet companies listed on the US stock market have hit astronomical valuations, with Amazon at US$1.4 trillion and Alphabet, Google's parent company, at close to US$1.5 trillion as of April 2022.[10] These massive numbers show the pervasive impact of the Internet and how it has become an indispensable part of our everyday lives.

---

[8] Statista, "Digital Economy Compass 2021," accessed April 26, 2022, https://www.statista.com/study/105653/digital-economy-compass, 21.

[9] Simon Kemp and DataReportal, "Digital 2022: Global Overview Report," January 26, 2022, https://datareportal.com/reports/digital-2022-global-overview-report.

[10] Yahoo Finance, "Amazon.com, Inc.," accessed April 26, 2022, https://finance.yahoo.com/quote/AMZN; Yahoo Finance, "Alphabet Inc.," accessed April 26, 2022, https://finance.yahoo.com/quote/GOOG.

Open-Access Ecosystem and Light-Touch Governance

There are two main features of the Internet we should note. The first is the open nature of its architecture from the viewpoint of access. Except for China and a few other countries, which have imposed a tight firewall around the World Wide Web, most other countries have kept the Web open for their citizens. This open access has brought many benefits, but one result is that there is no control over harmful or even unlawful content, as I will discuss shortly. A sensible middle road needs to be found, rather than an all-or-nothing approach.

A second feature is that the Internet is, by design, largely unregulated. There is no international Internet regulatory authority anywhere, nor is there any formal self-regulation structure. This light-touch governance has also spilled over to the oversight of Internet companies, including the big tech platforms whose reach is massive and hence have enormous power to do both good and harm. The US web platforms are specifically given a remarkable blanket legal immunity with respect to third-party content in Section 230 of the country's Communications Decency Act of 1996. The Section reads:

> *No provider or user of an interactive computer service shall be treated as the publisher or speaker of any information provided by another information content provider.*

This is not the most elegant prose but the meaning is clear and it is often referred to as "the 26 words that created the Internet".[11] This immunity provided by Section 230 is unique to the US. No one else — not the European nations, Canada, Japan nor other countries — has a similar statute in their laws. Because web platforms like Google and Facebook are global entities, it is difficult or even impossible for individual countries to regulate them.

Another area of light-touch governance, especially in the US, is antitrust leniency when it comes to Internet companies. I spoke earlier of the mergers

---

[11] Jeff Kosseff, *The Twenty-Six Words That Created the Internet* (New York: Cornell University Press, 2019), 3.

and acquisitions in the mid-2000s. Since then, there have been many more large acquisitions by the Internet giants, all of which were approved expeditiously even where anti-competitive concerns were evident *prima facie*. This has led to super-charged growth in company size, market concentration and massive stock market valuations. What we have now is a new era of corporate barons with largely unregulated power, although there have been instances of large fines imposed on them.

Self-regulation by Internet companies has also been, until recently, almost non-existent. The high-profile exceptions were when Facebook and Twitter banned Donald Trump on their platforms. The result is that the Internet is seen as the Wild West of profit-driven capitalism. Worse still, malevolent actors have exploited the open access of the Internet and its light-touch governance, with many getting away lightly or going unpunished. I will discuss this darker side of the Internet next.

Part II: The Darker Side of the Internet

I should answer this question first: Why am I focusing so much of my lecture on the darker side of the Internet? As I have explained, the Internet has without doubt brought many benefits to its users, as well as to companies, investors and the economy at large. But I want to shed light on the darker side of the Internet because my position is that not enough is being done to address the abuses and exploitation by bad actors in the Internet space.

As I said at the start, I genuinely believe that the global governance model is in urgent need of a deep review. The bigger danger is that it must not trigger another dot-com crash.

I am a big user of the Internet myself and have been for decades. So I am a fan, a genuine fan. My message is simply this: We must collectively deal with the bad actors and restore trust and integrity in the Internet system.

Let me list two specific concerns and I'll then speak more about them.

The first is the deluge of wilful misinformation that I spoke of at the start of my lecture. This also includes extremism and even subversion on Internet platforms. Let me clarify that I am not talking about mere views and opinions, which everyone is entitled to hold and express. I am talking about wilful factual misinformation.

The second issue is the scams, fraud and cybercrime which are now rampant in many parts of the Internet. I will later use, as a case study, the digital advertising ecosystem, to show how a beautiful system is being corrupted by fraudsters.

Wilful Misinformation

I will start with wilful misinformation. The issue is the harmful content that is swirling around the Internet. I come back again to the alleged Hillary Clinton paedophile ring. I recently read an investigative piece in *Rolling Stone* magazine where the reporter followed the digital trail and identified the person who posted this piece of fake news on her Facebook account under another name. Believe it or not, it was a 60-year-old attorney who practised law out of her home in Missouri. As I said earlier, in five weeks, her post was shared on Twitter 1.4 million times by a quarter million accounts. Nothing has happened to her and presumably she is still practising law.[12]

However, a 28-year-old man from North Carolina who read about the child sex ring drove all the way to the pizzeria in Washington, D.C. armed with an assault rifle to rescue the alleged kidnapped children. He found none, but fired three shots and subsequently was arrested, charged and jailed for four years.[13]

How is it that one committed a crime, and the other did not? The issue of course is freedom of expression. No matter how false the information, no matter what damage it causes or who ended up in jail, her freedom of expression was sacrosanct. Like it or not, that is the law in the US.

I now move to a related point: the reluctance of web platforms like Facebook to moderate content on their web platforms. I should clarify here that I am not talking about *prior* moderation. If Hillary Clinton, the

---

[12] Robb, "Anatomy of a Fake News Scandal."
[13] Ibid.

Presidential candidate, points out (with proof) that this story is false, should Facebook not have the moral duty, if not the legal responsibility, to take it down? Should that not apply to anyone who is maligned in a similar fashion as well?

Of course, here we come up against the aforementioned Section 230. On the one hand, we have absolute freedom of expression of the user, and on the other, complete legal immunity of the web platform. I hope lawmakers in the US will see that at the rate the deluge of wilful misinformation is growing — along with the polarisation in America and the growth of conspiracy theories — what is being endangered is American democracy itself.

To be fair, both Facebook and Twitter redeemed themselves somewhat when they booted Donald Trump from their platforms for persistently repeating his Big Lie that the last election was stolen. However, this is just a "whack-a-mole" strategy. What is needed is a fundamental relook at the law and a moderate middle road to address abuse.

The American political scientist Francis Fukuyama proposed an interesting idea in a recent *Foreign Affairs* article: create a layer of competitive "middleware" companies to which web platforms can outsource the job of moderating content.[14] It is an idea well worth considering as content moderation will be at an arm's length.

This is needed even more in non-English speaking developing countries, such as in Africa, where as a *Guardian* article put it, Facebook *is* the Internet. While it is indispensable for the everyday life of many Africans, Facebook's stance on moderation has led not just to abuse but violence and mayhem. In October last year, CNN reported that Facebook knew that its platform in Ethiopia was being used to incite violence, but it did not act.[15]

---

[14] Francis Fukuyama, Barak Richman, and Ashish Goel, "How to Save Democracy From Technology," *Foreign Affairs*, January/February 2021, https://www.foreignaffairs.com/articles/united-states/2020-11-24/fukuyama-how-save-democracy-technology?check_logged_in=1&utm_medium=promo_email&utm_source=lo_flows&utm_campaign=registered_user_welcome&utm_term=email_1&utm_content=20220422.

[15] Eliza Mackintosh, "Facebook Knew It Was Being Used to Incite Violence in Ethiopia. It Did Little to Stop the Spread, Documents Show," *CNN*, October 25, 2021, https://edition.cnn.com/2021/10/25/business/ethiopia-violence-facebook-papers-cmd-intl/index.html.

In Bangladesh, two incendiary posts on Facebook last year went viral and led to Muslims attacking hundreds of Hindu homes and temples.[16] In Myanmar, Rohingyas are suing Facebook, claiming that its algorithms "amplified hate speech against the Rohingya people" and that it "failed to invest in moderators."[17]

These cases raise two other areas of concern about the giant web platforms:

1. The rampant use of web robots, or bots, to broadcast misinformation or inflammatory content to ensure it goes viral.
2. Algorithm-based targeting which creates "echo chambers" of conspiracists, extremists and other polarised groups. Once they discern an interest, the algorithms pummel users with similar content.

Time does not permit me to elaborate on these concerns, but there need to be guideposts on the use of such tech devices. The tech giants that derive billions in Internet revenues need to work harder to find ways to stem the bad use of bots on the Internet.

A Case Study: Digital Advertising

My second concern has to do with scams, fraud and cybercrime, which have become rampant on the Internet. Rather than address each area, I will use digital advertising as a case study to highlight the issues.

Digital advertising on the Internet is a huge, data-driven, highly automated marketing ecosystem with thousands of players. But this is no ordinary ecosystem. As one writer, Tim Hwang, put it, digital advertising is "the beating heart of the business of the Internet".[18] He added that it is

---

[16] Subir Bhaumik, "Why Did Muslim Hardliners Attack Hindus in Bangladesh's Worst Bout of Communal Violence in Two Decades?" *South China Morning Post*, October 20, 2021, https://www.scmp.com/week-asia/politics/article/3153016/why-did-muslims-attack-hindus-bangladeshs-worst-bout-communal.

[17] "Rohingya Sue Facebook for $150bn Over Myanmar Hate Speech," *BBC*, December 7, 2021, https://www.bbc.com/news/world-asia-59558090.

[18] Tim Hwang, *Subprime Attention Crisis: Advertising and the Time Bomb at the Heart of the Internet* (New York: Farrar, Straus and Giroux, 2020), 11.

"impossible to think about the future of the Internet without thinking about the future of advertising."[19]

You have already seen how digital advertising powered the phenomenal growth of the tech giants. For them, their business is now almost wholly about digital advertising. According to Alphabet's 2021 annual report, 80 per cent of Google's revenues are derived from this one source.[20] For Facebook, it is a whopping 98 per cent.[21] Anyone who knows about corporate risk management will know how huge a business risk this is; their entire future is dependent on digital advertising.

In its early years, Google anticipated only about 10 to 15 per cent of its revenue would come from advertising.[22] The rest was assumed to come from licensing its search technology to other websites. Tim Hwang writes: "This was blown away by the torrent of money generated by advertising."[23]

We saw recently how the shares of Meta, Facebook's parent company, plunged by 26 per cent in a day and wiped out US$230 billion of its market capitalisation. One reason was that its advertising revenues were hit by changes that Apple made to the tracking of users on its devices.[24] This shows the market's sensitivity to advertising revenue numbers (in addition of course to the number of users).

Let me state my main point. Of the US$455 billion spent globally on digital advertising in 2021, 14 per cent of it was advertising fraud involving fake websites.[25] According to data collated by Statista, it is estimated that advertising fraud will hit US$100 billion by 2023. That is around 17 per cent

---

[19] Ibid., 28.

[20] Alphabet Inc., "Alphabet Annual Report 2021," accessed April 25, 2022, https://abc.xyz/investor/static/pdf/20220202_alphabet_10K.pdf?cache=fc81690, 33.

[21] Meta Investor Relations, "Facebook Reports Fourth Quarter and Full Year 2021 Results," February 2, 2022, https://investor.fb.com/investor-news/press-release-details/2022/Meta-Reports-Fourth-Quarter-and-Full-Year-2021-Results/default.aspx.

[22] Hwang, *Subprime Attention Crisis*, 56.

[23] Ibid.

[24] Lauren Feiner, "Facebook Stock Plummets 26% in its Biggest One-Day Drop Ever," *CNBC*, February 3, 2022, https://www.cnbc.com/2022/02/03/facebook-shares-plummet-22percent-after-reporting-weak-guidance.html.

[25] Ethan Cramer-Flood, "Worldwide Digital Ad Spending 2021," *eMarketer*, April 29, 2021, https://www.emarketer.com/content/worldwide-digital-ad-spending-2021; Statista, "Estimated cost of digital ad fraud worldwide," [2018–2023 data], September 14, 2021, https://www.statista.com/statistics/677466/digital-ad-fraud-cost.

of global digital advertising.[26] This is a colossal amount of fraud. The share is also growing, which means the problem is getting worse. I want to shed some light on where and how this fraud is happening.

The marketplace where the Internet demonstrates its true power is in what is called "programmatic ad buying." This is where advertisers can place orders to buy ad space from website owners through a computerised ad exchange that uses a real-time bidding system.

What happens is, the moment a reader clicks on a website, a signal is sent instantly to the ad exchange. The real-time bidding kicks in, and the highest bidder's ad is automatically uploaded onto that website.

The amazing thing is, this happens literally at the speed of light, before you can blink. It is truly a marvel of the digital revolution. Millions and millions of such transactions happen daily. In 2021, programmatic advertising in the US accounted for 90 per cent (US$97 billion) of total spending on digital display advertising.[27]

So where is the problem? The answer is, while the automation is brilliant, the rules of the game and the policing are not quite there. In other words, governance is totally missing.

According to data from 2017, 56 per cent of all advertising dollars in the programmatic space went to fake websites.[28] These are websites set up by fraudsters who make use of bots to create fake readers. All the audience traffic they report is "non-human traffic", as it is called in the trade. So, if an advertiser paid for $10,000 of advertising, less than half would go to genuine sites. The fraudsters with their fake websites would take the rest. Additionally, a 2018 survey of advertisement buyers and agencies found that 37 per cent of respondents cited advertising fraud as the most negative aspect of programmatic ad buying.[29]

---

[26] Ibid.

[27] Nicole Perrin, "Why Our Forecast of 2021 US Programmatic Digital Ad Spending is Now $15 Billion Higher," *eMarketer*, June 30, 2021, https://www.emarketer.com/content/forecast-2021-us-programmatic-digital-display-ad-spending-15-billion-higher.

[28] Hwang, *Subprime Attention Crisis*, 129.

[29] Marketing Charts, "Most Negative Aspects of Programmatic Ad Buying," July 2018, https://www.marketingcharts.com/charts/negative-aspects-programmatic-ad-buying.

Figure 3. Most Negative Aspects of Programmatic Ad Buying

% of Respondents Ranking each within Top 3, from a List of 10

Category	%
Fraud: Viewability, Non-human Traffic	~37%
Brand Safety Concerns	~36%
Poor Inventory Quality	~25%
Pricing Transparency and Hidden Costs	~23%
Data management complexity	~23%
Difficult to Measure Impact	~22%

Source: Adapted from MarketingCharts, "Most Negative Aspects of Programmatic Ad Buying," July 2018, https://www.marketingcharts.com/charts/negative-aspects-programmatic-ad-buying

You may well ask: Why does no one check whether a site is genuine or fake? Remember, the Internet is an open access system, where anyone can create a website. All you need is an IP address and a domain name. If you know how to write code and generate some bad bots, you can clock up as much non-human traffic as you need to fool the automated advertisement buying system.

What I do find hard to understand is why the brilliant automated system is so easily fooled, and why no one has found a way to shut out bad bots and non-human traffic. This is clearly an area where more needs to be done.

As of now, digital advertising is very much a "buyer beware" system. Unfortunately, many small companies in the long tail of advertisers — who account for an estimated 60 per cent of all ad spending — go in with their eyes closed. They are the ones who lose money to the fraudsters. Every intermediary in the ecosystem takes its cut, no matter where the advertising ends up. Now you can see why, when no one is policing the system, the players themselves have little incentive to fix the problem of fraud.

Fraudsters are now even copying the websites of quality publishers who charge premium prices for their ads. This is known as "domain spoofing".

In 2017, *Financial Times* (*FT*) discovered that crooks were selling fake *FT* impressions as well as video inventory they did not even have. The fake inventory was selling for US$1.3 million per month, which *FT*'s ad operations director described as "jaw dropping".[30] The difference here is that not only did the advertisers get skimmed but *FT* also lost revenue that it should have received.

For completeness, I should add that some advertising, such as video advertising, are charged by the number of clicks. Not surprisingly, "click fraud" has also become a widespread practice, either using bots or armies of paid humans in "click farms". According to Adobe, in 2018, 28 per cent of click traffic were from "non-human signals". For video advertisements, click fraud is 22 per cent.[31]

You can easily see that advertising fraud flourishes because of:

1. The sheer size of the digital advertising market.
2. The fact that it is highly lucrative.
3. How easy it is to make money through advertising fraud.
4. How easily malevolent actors can get away unpunished.

In 2018, *New York Times* profiled a so-called "entrepreneur" who in 18 months went from being on welfare and living with his father to buying a BMW and a house of his own, with earnings from advertising fraud.[32]

---

[30] Hwang, *Subprime Attention Crisis*, 131.

[31] Ibid., 129–130.

[32] Ibid., 150.

I will end my brief case study by saying that if fraud in digital advertising was of the order of 1 to 2 per cent, it could be written off as "friction" in the system. However, when the fraud level is 20 per cent, and as high as 50 per cent as it is in programmatic advertising, it is beyond unacceptable.

It is surely time for all players in the digital advertising ecosystem to rally together and collaborate to do more to fix the issues of fraud, the lack of transparency and bad bots. These should not be left to the ad tech companies to fix. All players — ad buyers, website owners, digital measurement players, etc. — must work together to develop effective solutions and set best practices for the industry. More can also be done to educate the long tail of small advertisers to be aware of the pitfalls of digital advertising.

Advertising fraud aside, there are a host of other much bigger problems, with serious consequences, such as cybercrime and cyberattacks, and some of which involve state-sponsored actors. Time does not permit me to address this here, but I shall be happy to take questions on this later.

Part III: What is the Way Forward for Internet Governance?

I would like to move now to the concluding part of my lecture. I had initially wanted to review the new regulatory moves affecting the Internet that are afoot in the US, Europe and elsewhere. I also wanted to review Singapore's early regulatory actions such as the Protection from Online Falsehoods and Manipulation Act (POFMA) and also discuss ideas for the future.

Instead, I decided to take a step back and discuss the broader issue of what the way forward for the global community is. For me, the issue is governance. I am not referring to regulation by governments, although this is surely a part of the challenge and solution. What seems clear to me is that a broader collaborative approach is needed. I agree with those who say that this is one of the most pressing public policy issues of our time. I do not have the prescriptions, but I can try to outline the issues and what the options might be.

Some six years ago, in 2016, our Foreign Minister Vivian Balakrishnan gave a thoughtful speech at a security conference. He was Minister-in-Charge of Singapore's Smart Nation Initiative and spoke about the need to "embark on deep policy reviews on very difficult topics", one of them being the Internet. I would like to quote him at some length.

> *You see, the problem is in the initial euphoric days of the establishment of the Internet. There were many people who dreamt of a completely free and unregulated space, with absolute freedom to say anything, the ability to transact secretly across borders, and to mobilise people for any cause without interference or being watched by security agencies. This was the dream of some of the early pioneers of the Internet.*
>
> *But I believe there is a false dichotomy between the real world and the cyber world. I believe we actually only have one world — a technology-enabled world and what goes on in cyberspace has real impact on the real world, and the sooner we get to grips with these difficult policy issues the better, because we need to get the balance right... we actually live in a more unsettled world.*[33]

I agree fully with Dr Balakrishnan. We only have one world, and we must get the balance right. The sooner we deal with the difficult issues of governance the better, as we live in troubled times.

Possible Future Scenarios

I also studied a 2016 report by the Global Commission on Internet Governance, titled "One Internet". The headline of its summary was: "The

---

[33] Vivian Balakrishnan, "Edited Transcript of Opening Address by Minister for Foreign Affairs Dr Vivian Balakrishnan at the 10th Asia-Pacific Programme for Senior National Security Officers on April 11, 2016, 9am at the Marina Mandarin," *Ministry of Foreign Affairs*, https://www.mfa.gov.sg/Newsroom/Press-Statements-Transcripts-and-Photos/2016/04/Edited-Transcript-of-Opening-Address-by-Minister-for-Foreign-Affairs-Dr-Vivian-Balakrishnan-at-the-1.

future of the Internet hangs in the balance." It confidently said: "The Internet as we know it ... will not be the Internet of the future."[34]

It went on to outline three possible future scenarios, from the worst case to the ideal:

1. **Worst-case scenario: A dangerous and broken cyberspace**
   This is one where "the Internet breaks on our watch". The breakdown is brought about by a combination of malicious actions of criminals and inadvertent effects of government regulation of the Internet. People simply stop using the Internet and its potential is lost.
2. **Second scenario: Stunted growth, uneven and unequal gains**
   Here, some users "capture a disproportionate share of 'digital dividends'" while others are locked out, but the world muddles along.
3. **The ideal scenario: Broad unprecedented progress**
   This scenario sees the adoption of new Internet-enabled technologies such as driverless cars and blockchain. Governments and industries act collaboratively across borders to manage the risks of online activity, and ensure that the Internet is open, secure, trustworthy and inclusive for everyone.

It concludes by saying the optimistic future can only be achieved if there is, and I quote, "universal agreement to collectively develop a new social compact" on the Internet.[35]

I am afraid I am not at all optimistic about a new universal social compact. Just the geopolitics alone will scupper any attempt to achieve this. It will also expose the fundamental differences between those whose constitutional bedrock is untrammelled freedom of expression and those who believe in freedom with caveats, let alone those who will never let go of totalitarian control.

---

[34] Centre for International Governance Innovation and Chatham House, "Preface," in *Global Commission on Internet Governance: One Internet* (2016), 9–10, https://www.cigionline.org/static/documents/gcig_final_report_-_with_cover.pdf.

[35] Ibid.

My guess would be that we will end up with a scenario that is a jumble of all three scenarios: parts of the Internet will be broken, but the world muddles along with unequal gains, while at the same time there will also be adoption of new Internet-enabled technologies like driverless vehicles and blockchain.

Charting Our Own Way Forward

What this unfortunately means is that Singapore will have to chart its own way forward, guided by its own circumstances. In doing this, it must strive to get the maximum "digital dividends" through well-thought-out Internet governance.

I would recommend these guideposts:

1. We need a balanced and collaborative approach to Internet governance.
2. We need to build a society that is resilient to adverse Internet influences.
3. We need to stay focused on the goal of an Internet that is open, secure, trustworthy and inclusive for all our citizens and residents.

This is the challenge of Internet governance that we face. As I said, it is urgent that we begin to address this as a country and as a society.

Question-and-Answer Session
Moderated by Dr Carol Soon

Mr Patrick Daniel and Dr Carol Soon at the Q&A session
Source: Jacky Ho for the Institute of Policy Studies

Dr Carol Soon: Thank you, Patrick, for the lecture. I will use my privilege as moderator to ask the first question. The main thrust of your lecture today looks at the governance of cyberspace and the Internet. Clearly, as you mentioned earlier, when the Internet was first launched and when it proliferated, the assumptions that many people had of the Internet and its possible impact on society were very utopic. People believed that the Internet would provide an equal playing field for different people and different groups, like marginalised political parties, for instance. We have obviously seen in the past decades how that has not really worked out. And certainly, in the past five years when the problems of fake news, misinformation and disinformation became more evident, we saw the vulnerabilities of the Internet.

You talked about regulation and you talked about governance. I think that there is general agreement in many parts of the community that regulation is quite important. The space cannot be an unfettered free-for-all, or else it will become the Wild West that we sometimes see in the online space. We can also see how different countries are trying to, as you said earlier, find the "middle way" to regulate the Internet. Closer to home, we see efforts made by Vietnam, Thailand and of course Singapore. Like you alluded to earlier, Singapore has recently, in the past three to four years, rolled out two laws.[36] We also see some attempts at regulation in South Asia and further away in Europe.

I think regulation is complicated by two things. First, there is the complexity of the cyberspace, and second there is also the rapid speed at which technology is advancing. As such, regulation is always playing catch-up. If we look at the next big thing, which everybody has been talking about, it is the Metaverse. But interestingly, as it is being built, people are already starting to pay attention to the kind of structures that need to be put in place to protect and govern the space. This approach is very different from what it used to be, which was "build first and regulate later".

So what makes for sustainable governance? What should the first principles be? If you could pick three values for sustainable governance, what would they be?

Mr Patrick Daniel: The first thing is that it has to remain open, which is how it was first developed. Of course, the other extreme is China, which decided that there would be no World Wide Web for the Chinese.

The second value for me is that it has to be secure. That means there has to be some policing of bad actors, crooks and criminals. For them,

---

[36] The two laws are the Protection from Online Falsehoods and Manipulation Act (POFMA) and the Foreign Interference (Countermeasures) Act (FICA).

compared to the real world, the digital world is easy money. Security is an important feature.

The third thing I would say, which is related to security and being secure, is trustworthiness. I would say at least these three values. This is the consensus among academics. In fact, they have four — openness, security, trustworthiness and the last one is inclusivity. You must aim to include everybody. You do not want a system that is very bourgeois and where only the educated know how to get in and the rest do not. It has to be inclusive and allow everybody to come in.

But it is easier said than done, because you have to get people to agree on where the controls must be and why policing is needed. There has to be some surveillance, otherwise how do you police it? There are people who just do not agree with surveillance. So, it is going to be a very difficult exercise, especially when there is no international consensus.

Actually, the Internet is one of the few things that was developed as a global product and a global service with no governance at all. I will give you an example. Imagine air travel with no governance — planes flying and landing all over the place. It is just not possible. You need to have a regulatory authority that decides who looks after what, making sure everybody is well trained and that planes land properly. Look at how beautifully it is managed. There are thousands of airplanes flying all over the place. It is very well managed and generally very well organised.

The Internet was, as Minister Vivian Balakrishnan pointed out, invented by dreamers who decided that it would be open to everybody without any need for governance. I remember in one of the papers that I read, Tim Berners-Lee, the man who invented the World Wide Web, had believed it had to be open and he did not patent anything. His HTML software was free for everybody. You could put up your website using his software. It is just wonderful, and such a generous thing to do. But he now also believes that we might need a little bit of regulation. He did not say exactly what regulation, but I think people are coming around to it. However, I think large parts of our population will have to be brought around to it, because there are lots of people who love the anonymity of the Internet. You say what you like and nobody knows who you are. So, it is going to be very hard to pull back once you have such a free and open system.

Dr Soon: I asked for three values and you gave me four, thank you very much. They are: be open, secure, trustworthy and inclusive, right? We have a question from a participant who is joining us online. His question is related to your last value on inclusion. He asked: What does an inclusive Internet mean to you? How should, or how would that look like and who are excluded? What do we do with them? I think you briefly touched on that, but would you like to say more?

Mr Daniel: Inclusivity just means that anybody who wants to use the Internet can use it. It is as simple as that. You should not exclude anybody. If you have a system where a 10-year-old cannot come in, that is not inclusive. You want it to be open to everybody. However, if a 10-year-old uses the Internet, the parents must be able to decide what and when to switch on and switch off. I use inclusiveness in the common meaning of the word. Nothing more than that. Anybody should be able to use the Internet, which is happening now. It is quite inclusive. In Singapore, everybody is on their handphones surfing the Web, talking to people, Skyping. That is what I mean by inclusive, and I think the future Internet should remain that way.

Dr Soon: An important point that I picked up from your response is that when we talk about inclusiveness, it is not just about access anymore. Because increasingly, we see fewer issues — not that there are no issues — when it comes to having physical access to technology or the Internet. I think the mobile smartphone is one big contributor. Because of its low cost and its small size, it has basically made access to the Internet a lot easier. But increasingly, and you hinted at that, inclusion is also about people's ability and competency in using technology to enhance their economic and social mobility.

Going back to regulation, we have two questions here on different countries' approaches. The first question is what your views on China's actions are when it comes to regulation. Do you see China's regulation as a genuine attempt at achieving good Internet balance or do you see its regulatory attempt as a draconian regulation as the West likes to put it?

Mr Daniel: It is quite a recent firewall. The problem I see is how do you open up? It will be very difficult for a future leader to open up the Internet and the World Wide Web for China. The critics will say it is like Gorbachev trying to achieve glasnost and perestroika. After that, the whole country fell apart. So it is going to be very hard to unwind. It is easy to put up the firewall but very hard to unwind. It is of course one way to address all the negatives that I mentioned about the Internet. I did not mention things like pornography, cybercrime and cyberattacks. China decided that it would have its own Internet within the country that all its 1.4 billion people can access freely.

This is why international Internet governance is going to be so difficult. The Chinese have one view, the Americans have another, and the Europeans have a slightly different view. I do not have a definitive view on whether Chinese regulations are draconian or not. I am just saying that the Chinese government believes that security and stability are far more important than access to the World Wide Web. The Chinese are very digitally savvy, they are far savvier than us. They never carry cash and they pay for everything online through their phones. But to get into the World Wide Web, you need a roundabout way using a VPN. Is that good for their country? I do not know — they have to decide that for themselves. My view is that I think it is better to be open. But I see a great difficulty for China to open up. They can do it slowly, but it will not be inclusive as it means that only certain segments will benefit. Those are just my thoughts. No great wisdom in what I am saying.

Dr Soon: Coming back to Singapore, we have a question. In your opinion, should the Singapore government also roll out regulations against the big tech companies? What do you think are the pros and cons for a small city-state like us? Let me provide a preamble. We do have certain regulations in place. You mentioned the POFMA. That, among other provisions, enabled the government to issue targeted corrective directions as well as general corrective directions. We have seen that used on tech platforms such as Facebook. What is your opinion? Should the Singapore government roll out more regulations against big tech companies? Given our economic status as a hub, what do you think the pros and cons are?

Mr Daniel: That is a challenge. As I said in my lecture, they are global companies. POFMA was a very interesting test to see if Facebook would take something down if it were told to do so. And if they did not take it down, what would be done then? Would the government shut Facebook down and leave the whole of Singapore unable to use it? So it is a real challenge.

It is a good experiment on whether or not individual countries can regulate global platforms. When Australia tried to negotiate payments for their newspapers using their News Media and Digital Platforms Mandatory Bargaining Code, the platforms responded very negatively initially.[37] And then, they settled. So, it is not a given that tech platforms will just roll over and do what you say, because they know they may shut down the population that is reliant on their platforms. It is not an easy thing to do but it is possible to apply reasonable laws.

I have come to the view that there is just so much crime online that if you want to make these platforms secure, you cannot leave them alone just because they are global companies. I think you have to find a way to regulate in a balanced way. We have to bring the platforms in, talk to them and see how to deal with the problems before finding an acceptable solution. Take online banking. To deal with the scams, you have to bring in the various

---

[37] The News Media and Digital Platforms Mandatory Bargaining Code is a mandatory code to help support the sustainability of public interest journalism in Australia. It does this by addressing bargaining power imbalances between digital platforms and Australian news businesses. The code enables eligible news businesses to bargain individually or collectively with digital platforms over payment for the inclusion of news on the platforms and services.

players, including the telecommunication companies, to deal with the crime syndicates. This was how our Ministry of Home Affairs was quite quick to catch the recent OCBC scammers. You do need that kind of policing — to use a tough word — and that policing has to be on the Internet as well. I am open to having some surveillance, because otherwise you cannot do anything and deserve to be scammed. So that is my long answer.

Dr Soon: Towards the end of your lecture, in your take on what needs to be done, you spoke about adopting a collaborative approach to governing the Internet and you also just mentioned that in your response. One way that is being explored right now, is what some researchers are calling the "middle way", where governments work closely with tech platforms to come up with guidelines that are suited for individual countries' contexts, given the very different values and ideologies that underpin different societies. I think that could be a possible road to take in collaborating and working together to make the Internet a better and more egalitarian space for all.

Here is the last question on regulation, because I want to speak with you on something else next. One participant is quite concerned about the regulation that benefits everyone and does not privilege a few people. Given the power dynamics behind regulation-making, how do we ensure that regulations benefit all rather than privilege the powerful few?

Mr Daniel: I do not see that as an issue in Singapore. I cannot think of any regulation that benefits the powerful and not everybody. I think our laws are quite plain. If you break the law, you will be punished regardless of who you are. I am not quite sure I understand what his mental frame is when he poses that question. I think that if any minister puts up a law that benefits the few, it will not pass. I think even the People's Action Party Members of Parliament will tell the Minister so. I think that is more of an intellectual worry than a real worry, if I may be honest.

Dr Soon: We have quite an interesting suggestion here. It says: A common point of agreement for most people would be the need to protect our youths from the harms of the Internet. Do you think that this would be a good starting point for discussions on governance and regulation? What thoughts do you have on what can be done to protect our young people?

Mr Daniel: When I say security is one value to focus on for regulation, I actually do have the young in mind. There are already many websites that worry me. Websites like Roblox, for example, where young people have an avatar and are able to, say, buy a pair of jeans for their avatar using real money or crypto. Young people are actually already transacting on the early Metaverse. Youths are doing it and they are paying. There is no regulation of this. I do not mind if Roblox themselves set some rules and did a monthly billing, but there is nothing.

I worry about the young and I think if you want to find an area where there is broad consensus, it is the young. I think that whichever side of the political fence you are on, if you come up with rules to protect the young, there will be majority agreement. So yes, I agree with him. A good friend of mine just told me yesterday that he knows of somebody who trades in the Non-Fungible Token (NFT) market, and it is scary how much money is involved. It is big money. You take a photo of your cat, you put it up, and you can sell it. It is just amazing. I do worry about the kids.

Dr Soon: Perhaps another important first principle when thinking about governance or legislation is whom we are trying to protect. We should start with that very important fundamental question.

I would like to move away from the regulation and governance of platforms and connect some of the points that you made today with your first lecture. We have talked about platforms on one end, but of course, on the other is a very big stakeholder that is the audience — the users of the Internet.

During your first lecture, you talked about the need to invest in technology and talent to strengthen the media industry and make it more sustainable. I would say that talent and technology are very tangible assets. There is also a very important asset that is not so tangible — trust. More specifically, audience trust. If we look at the *Reuters* Digital News Report that was published last year, it seems that things bode quite well for news media. For example, one of the key findings is that trust in news in general has gone up. The other finding is the trust gap has widened — between news in general and news from aggregated environments, such as news from social media. How do you think the media can maintain its lead in the trust gap?

Mr Daniel: You just have to make trust one of your principal values and make sure that you do not damage the trust. In fact, much of what I am saying about the Internet also holds true for the legacy media. Trust is very hard to regain when it is lost. You have to be factual and you have to make sure that your reporters behave ethically. You have to make that a value of the organisation. That is what we are trying to do at the SPH Media Trust. We want to be accurate and correct our mistakes, so that people know that if something appears in *The Straits Times*, it must be true. We are getting there. People believe our stories when we report, so that is a good thing. I have not read that *Reuters* survey yet, but you are right. Apart from talent and technology, if you lose the audience's trust you are in deep trouble.

Dr Soon: We have just five minutes left and I would like to take this opportunity to ask one last question. We talked about the cyberspace, and another very important feature of the cyberspace is fragmentation. Fragmentation happens because people generally have the freedom to seek out different information sources and go to different websites that they want to visit. The fact is that the Internet's natural infrastructure allows new monopolies to form very naturally. It is a place where we see how the winner-takes-most phenomenon plays out very clearly. The biggest sites and platforms attract most of the eyeballs.

Let me link this back to the news industry. Clearly, the news media industry is more than just legacy or traditional media. Increasingly, we see how new players or entrepreneurial media play a very important part in different societies. For instance, in the context of Australia, media entrepreneurs play a very important part in filling the void in news deserts in Australia. This refers to places or communities that are not well served by legacy media. Similarly, in many other societies, small media players play a very important part in providing alternative perspectives. What are your thoughts on how we can encourage and nurture smaller, independent players in the media?

Mr Daniel: For local news in many countries, there is already government support so that small communities are well served by their newspapers. Many of the legacy media outlets have closed because they were bought up by big groups. But when they became unprofitable, they were shut down. I have no disagreement with smaller independent newspapers being funded whether by the government or by a trust, because you do need to have that.

For example, someone wants to start "Toa Payoh News" and this person is a professional journalist and has a business plan. I think that funding this entrepreneurial organisation is good. As a newspaperman, I do want people to read the news because it is important to know what is going on and to be aware. To me, anything that promotes reading current affairs is a good thing. I have no issue with that. However, there must be some standards. The person must understand what professional journalism is.

I have a story to tell. I was once interviewed by a website after speaking at a conference. When the piece was published, my daughter called me and was shocked by some of the quotes that had been attributed to me. I checked and was shocked too. I called the journalist up and asked if he had a record of me saying what he claimed I said. He told me that he did not have any notes or a record. I asked him how he managed to quote me for several paragraphs — he had it in quotes. His response was: he had a good memory of what I said. This is just not professional journalism, and I told him so. There are untrained people who think that journalism is very easy.

People who want to start news media outlets need to know what journalism is. I think there must be some standards. I am not trying to be elitist. I am just saying journalism is a profession and there must be some standards of what you can do and what you should not do. On social media, people talk without checking what is true and what is not true. You must check your facts. That is my long answer.

Dr Soon: Thank you, Patrick. I think we hear you loud and clear. Support can be given, but there should be some standards that guide the business and how news is made. We have actually gone past the time that we were given. Thank you for sharing with us your thoughts on Internet governance and also proposing some of the key values that should underpin sustainable governance.

Lecture III
ENVISIONING DESIRED FUTURES FOR SINGAPORE AND FOR THE LOCAL MEDIA

LECTURE III

In my first lecture, I looked at Singapore's media history and how the legacy media was severely disrupted by the Internet revolution. In my second lecture, I spoke about the need for a greater global effort in Internet governance. Today, I want to look forward and try to envision desired futures for Singapore and for the legacy media here.

I started preparing for this third lecture by wanting to look ahead to 2045 when Singapore celebrates its 80th anniversary of Independence. It so happens that *The Straits Times* (*ST*) will celebrate its 200th anniversary that year. So, 2045 is a good date on my 20-year horizon. I wanted to ask: Which trends will profoundly affect Singapore's future as a society? And also, what would it take for *ST* and our legacy media to thrive past 2045?

I found out quickly that it is not easy to be a futurist. I should rephrase that: It is not easy to take the guesswork out of being an amateur futurist. After speaking to people with experience in scenario planning and strategic futures, I learnt about an alternative method, which I want to use today. It is called "backcasting".

Backcasting vs Forecasting

Let me explain what backcasting is. Simply put, it is the opposite of forecasting. In forecasting, you start from the present, you study today's trends and then project into the future.

In backcasting, you start by asking what is your *desired* future? You put yourself in that desired future and from there look backward, or backcast, to the present. You then plot the discrete steps you need to take to get to your desired future.

Truth be told, if this sounds like pop psychology, you are not wrong. It does sound like the old saying, "Begin with the end in mind." Some of us remember Stephen Covey's book 30 years ago, *The 7 Habits of Highly Effective People*. It was Covey's Habit Number 2.[1]

That advice has a much longer history — going back to the Roman Stoic philosopher, Seneca, who in the first century AD wrote a work called *On the Tranquility of the Mind*. His words in Latin translate to: "Let all your effort be directed towards a particular aim and keep that aim in sight."[2]

Let me get back to the modern iteration. The primary elements of the backcasting method were outlined in the 1980s by a Canadian professor, John B. Robinson. He published a paper in 1988 which he titled "Unlearning and Backcasting: Rethinking Some of the Questions We Ask About the Future".

In his abstract, Robinson says:

> *In most cases, we ask the wrong questions when we forecast. What are needed are backcasting techniques that reveal the possibility of alternative futures. The focus thus shifts from prediction and likelihood, to feasibility and choice.*[3]

---

[1] Stephen R. Covey, *The 7 Habits of Highly Effective People: 30th Anniversary Edition* (New York: Simon & Schuster, 2020), 250.

[2] Lucius Annaeus Seneca, "On the Tranquility of the Mind," in *Oxford World's Classics: Seneca: Dialogues and Essays*, eds. John Davie and Tobias Reinhardt (Oxford: Oxford University Press, 2007), 132.

[3] John B. Robinson, "Unlearning and Backcasting: Rethinking Some of the Questions We Ask About the Future," *Technological Forecasting and Social Change* 33, no. 4 (July 1988): 325–38.

So the keywords in backcasting are the following: (1) alternative futures, (2) feasibility and (3) choice.

A Thought Exercise in Backcasting

To better grasp this method, let me suggest a brief thought exercise by applying backcasting to something current — the situation in Ukraine in which the North Atlantic Treaty Organization (NATO) finds itself. Indulge me, for a moment.

Imagine if NATO had done a backcasting exercise immediately after the fall of the Berlin Wall in 1989 and the subsequent fall of the whole Iron Curtain. What desired futures would NATO have envisioned for it back then?

As a side note, what I am doing here is backcasting the backcasting exercise. I guess I am taking a leaf from Francis Fukuyama who has himself noted that the current events have been dubbed "The End of The End of History".[4] Amen to that.

Going back to NATO's choices. One choice in 1990 for NATO was to expand and admit whichever of the former Soviet republics that wanted to join the community of liberal democratic nations in Europe. Another choice was to heed those who belong to the realist school of international relations, who counselled greater care in dealing with the weakened superpower in the neighbourhood.

Both are valid desired futures. And you could do the same backcasting exercise for Ukraine and also Russia. I will leave you to complete these exercises, but I will highlight one obvious lesson: you have to be careful what you wish for as your desired future. This is especially so when you are experiencing the flush of victory or the shame of defeat.

Let me leave it there and move to the question of Singapore's desired futures.

---

[4] Francis Fukuyama, "Putin's War on the Liberal Order," *The Straits Times*, March 9, 2022, https://www.straitstimes.com/opinion/putins-war-on-the-liberal-order.

Desired Futures for Singapore

There are many dimensions to a country's desired future — geopolitics, domestic politics, the climate crisis, the economy and just about every sector of society.

I was happy to see a headline in *The Business Times* on Singapore's net-zero carbon ambition. The goal was moved from the second half of the century to "by or around mid-century".[5] Together with the bold carbon tax increases announced in the Budget, this is an excellent example of backcasting. The planners put themselves in the mid-century, chose their desired future (i.e., net-zero carbon emissions) and then worked out the carbon taxes needed now.

The Budget debate also saw several other transformative moves. The Singapore Armed Forces' new Digital and Intelligence Service, alongside the Army, Navy and Air Force, is another example.

But the question is how will it add up to a desired future as a country? What would be the composite picture?

The Singapore Pledge

As I thought about this question, I came to the view that Singapore's founding fathers envisioned in 1966 a remarkably clear desired future when they crafted the pledge that all Singaporean students still recite daily.

The Singapore pledge contains three main elements:

1. One united people, regardless of race, language or religion.
2. A democratic society, based on justice and equality.
3. Happiness, prosperity and progress for the nation.

This was an exceptional exercise in envisioning the future. The Singapore pledge, or at least its draft, is correctly attributed to S. Rajaratnam, the Foreign Minister at the time. But interestingly, it was the Education

---

[5] Annabeth Leow, "Decisive Net-Zero Shift Will Establish Singapore's Economic Chops: Teo Chee Hean," *The Business Times*, March 9, 2022, https://www.businesstimes.com.sg/government-economy/decisive-net-zero-shift-will-establish-singapores-economic-chops-teo-chee-hean-0.

Ministry that proposed the idea in October 1965. The Education Minister then, Ong Pang Boon, sent two different drafts to Rajaratnam, who applied his considerable skills and sent back a stronger third draft. The final version was approved in August 1966 after further substantive changes by the Cabinet.[6]

No timeframe was set for the pledge. It was an open-ended effort to promote national unity and consciousness. A pressing worry was to overcome divisions of race, language and religion.

One thing we can quickly agree on is that the Singapore pledge has remarkably stood the test of time. So, if we now do a backcasting exercise over a 20-year horizon, the pledge would be an excellent place to start. The task of updating our desired future would be to see where and how the pledge should be modified or added to, to take in new priorities and challenges.

A United People

First is the goal of being a united people, and not one riven by race, language or religion. In Rajaratnam's draft, the words he used were for Singaporeans to "*forget differences* of race, language and religion and become one united people".[7] Looking at how policies in this key area have since developed, it is not surprising to me that Rajaratnam's suggested wording was changed. The emphasis has been to create not a Singaporean race but a Singaporean identity, where all groups can rightfully retain their culture, language and religion. In my view, it was an inspired choice to be a multi-cultural society.

But there are already calls to drop the categorisation of "CMIO" (Chinese, Malay, Indian and Others). This needs a further debate on whether "forgetting differences" should or should not be part of the new desired

---

[6] National Heritage Board, "National Pledge," accessed May 6, 2022, https://www.nhb.gov.sg/what-we-do/our-work/community-engagement/education/resources/national-symbols/national-pledge; Zhi Wei and Kartini Saparudin, "National Pledge," *Singapore Infopedia*, August 1, 2014, https://eresources.nlb.gov.sg/infopedia/articles/SIP_84_2004-12-13.html.

[7] Wei and Saparudin, "National Pledge."

future. On this, a further observation I would make is, there are also intra-ethnic differences, as well as differing perspectives between new citizens and citizens born here.

This brings me to my key point. There are now many more differences in our society than just race, language and religion. One key dimension, I would argue, is domestic political differences. Singapore is increasingly becoming a politically diverse society — with "men (and women) in white", and those in blue and other colours. How to remain united in the face of this political diversity will require some deep thinking. The seriousness of this challenge is evident in the political polarisation we see in so many democracies, the prime example being the United States.

Yet another dimension is sexual orientation and gender identity. The last few decades have seen dramatic changes in global attitudes and acceptance of the lesbian, gay, bisexual, transgender and queer (LGBTQ) community. A survey carried out by the Institute of Policy Studies in 2018 showed that there is greater social acceptance of the LGBTQ community in Singapore as compared with 2013.[8] However, while social acceptance has grown, divisions remain between liberals and conservatives, mainly on religious grounds. Changes in official positions, over Section 377A of our Penal Code, for example, have therefore been deliberate, to manage these divisions. In fact, the divide in values between liberals and conservatives is a broader one that cuts across many other issues.

These other differences will need to be part of any new formulation of "one united people".

Equality and Inclusivity

I move to a second area: equality in our society. There are many aspects to this — equal rights, equal treatment, equality before the law, gender equality and so on. But the two key ones are equality of opportunities and equality of outcomes.

---

[8] Mathew Mathews, Leonard Lim, and Shanthini Selvarajan, "Religion, Morality and Conservatism in Singapore," *IPS Working Papers No.* 34 (May 2019): 62–63.

Equality of opportunities has all along been integral to Singapore's ideology. Upward social mobility has been high as a result. As Senior Minister Tharman Shanmugaratnam has put it, social mobility must be "at the heart and soul of our ambition for the future".[9]

However, inequality of outcomes remains an issue, with growing societal pressures for measures like wealth taxes and minimum wages to close the gap and create a more equal society. The 9th S R Nathan Fellow, Ravi Menon, covered this in his July 2021 lecture on being an inclusive society. Let me quote him:

> *Inequality of outcomes reflects inequality of ability and effort, and luck. An equal society will not be seen as just or fair by most people.*[10]

He continued:

> *I believe what most of us want instinctively is an inclusive society — one that provides broadly equal opportunity for all to move up in life; one that leaves no one behind; one that treats all with dignity and respect; in short, one that makes everyone feel included.*[11]

I think we can agree quite quickly that both social mobility and inclusivity must be part of our new desired future.

But this still does not quite resolve the problem of inequality of outcomes. I would like to take a moment to digress and share my views on this.

---

[9] Tharman Shanmugaratnam, "DPM Tharman Shanmugaratnam's Dialogue at the IPS 30th Anniversary Event," edited Transcript of the Dialogue on October 25, 2018, https://www.pmo.gov.sg/Newsroom/dpm-tharmans-dialogue-ips-30th-anniversary-event.

[10] Ravi Menon, *The Singapore Synthesis: Innovation, Inclusion, Inspiration* (Singapore: World Scientific Publishing, 2022), 88.

[11] Ibid.

Minimum Wages

First, minimum wages. I support a minimum wage in principle and spirit. However, I struggle with whether and how a minimum wage would work for a city-state like Singapore.

My concerns have to do with two special factors about Singapore:

1. We have a very high proportion of migrant workers.

Of the 1.2 million foreigners in our workforce (as of December 2021), 850,000 are work permit holders, which include 246,000 domestic workers.[12] By comparison, according to the Ministry of Manpower's 2021 report on the labour force in Singapore, our resident workforce is nearly 2.4 million.[13] Of this, 655,000 (about a quarter) have only secondary education or lower.[14]

2. We are surrounded by countries with surplus labour, especially at the lower-skilled end. The potential supply is, therefore, huge.

My assumption is that any nationally mandated minimum wage must apply equally to migrant workers. Many proponents of minimum wages seem to have elided over this point. Both the International Labour Organization (ILO) and the United Nations (UN) have adopted the position that, in respect of remuneration, all migrant workers have the right to enjoy treatment no less favourable than the nationals of the country.[15]

Given this, no self-respecting labour-exporting country would allow their migrant workers to be paid less than what the residents are entitled to by law. Simply put, if Singapore adopts a national minimum monthly wage of, say, S$1,200, this has to be paid to all our migrant workers too,

---

[12] Ministry of Manpower, "Foreign Workforce Numbers," [2016–2021 data], last updated March 16, 2022, https://www.mom.gov.sg/documents-and-publications/foreign-workforce-numbers

[13] Ministry of Manpower, Manpower Research & Statistics Department, "Resident Labour Force Aged Fifteen Years and Over by Highest Qualification Attained and Sex, 2011–2021 (June)," [2011–2021 data], released on January 28, 2022, https://stats.mom.gov.sg/iMAS_Tables1/LabourForce/LabourForce_2021/mrsd_2021LabourForce_T8.xlsx.

[14] Ibid.

[15] International Labour Organization, "Sub-Minimum Wages for Migrant Workers," accessed May 6, 2022, https://www.ilo.org/global/topics/wages/minimum-wages/rates/WCMS_451251/lang--en/index.htm; United Nations, "International Convention on the Protection of the Rights of All Migrant Workers and Members of Their Families," 10, accessed May 6, 2022, https://www.ohchr.org/sites/default/files/cmw.pdf.

including domestic workers. The first impact is a huge cost to the economy.

Furthermore, a Singapore minimum wage will surely be higher than the going wage for low-skilled workers in their home countries. If the gap is large, the number of migrant workers wanting jobs here, at our minimum wage, will far exceed our capacity to absorb them. This demand and supply imbalance will lead to a host of problems such as illegal workers and middlemen who extort huge commissions. Policing a minimum wage system will not be a trivial task. For domestic workers, if they have to be paid the Singapore minimum wage, employers might charge for board and lodge. Imagine the disputes this will lead to.

It would be far better, in my view, for Singapore to pursue other approaches to help our own low-wage workers. One safety net, a Singapore invention, is the Workfare Income Supplement (WIS) scheme established in 2007. This is an excellent scheme, targeted at citizens only, where the WIS tops up the monthly salary of low-wage workers by up to 30 per cent.

Initially, the WIS benefited 300,000 local workers.[16] The scheme was enhanced in 2020, and now almost 500,000 workers are beneficiaries. The government pays out S$850 million a year, and this is set to grow further.[17] A Ministry of Trade and Industry study found that the WIS has incentivised the less educated and the elderly to enter and remain in the workforce.[18]

Clearly, the WIS can be the centrepiece of Singapore's low-wage support policy. The other Singapore invention, the Progressive Wage Model — a tripartite effort by unions, employers and government to help lower-wage workers get wage increases through skills upgrading — can be an important additional support scheme.

---

[16] Ministry of Manpower, "Factsheet — Workfare Income Supplement," 2010, https://www.mom.gov.sg/-/media/mom/documents/speeches/2010/factsheet---wis-(110310).pdf.

[17] Lee Hsien Loong, "National Day Rally 2021," delivered August 29, 2021, https://www.pmo.gov.sg/Newsroom/National-Day-Rally-2021-English.

[18] Ministry of Trade and Industry, "Feature Article: The Impact of the Workfare Income Supplement Scheme on Individuals' Labour Outcomes," 30, August 12, 2014, https://www.mti.gov.sg/-/media/MTI/Legislation/Public-Consultations/2014/The-Impact-Of-The-Workfare-Income-Supplement-Scheme-on-Individuals-Labour-Outcomes/fa_2q14.pdf?la=en&hash=A04FA8D339AD599621D8ADE1AE06BAF3.

A separate point is that it might be a good idea to tie the WIS to wealth taxes, so that Singaporeans can see that wealth is being redistributed in a purposeful way. This will go some way to addressing unhappiness over the issue of inequality.

Wealth Taxes

This brings me to wealth taxes. One part of Ravi Menon's lecture in fact raised a bit of a kerfuffle, among some in our wealth management industry. This was when he said that to promote an inclusive society, it might make sense to shift our tax structure away from taxing income towards taxing wealth. A wealth tax, he added, could take the form of either a property gains tax or an inheritance tax (which was abolished in 2008).[19] That disturbed some people.

In February 2022, Finance Minister Lawrence Wong spelt out the government's policy on wealth taxes in his Budget Statement. What he said is worth quoting at some length.[20]

> [Wealth taxes are] an important part of our tax system. Apart from generating revenue, they ... mitigate social inequalities. Wealth taxes are therefore needed to build a fairer society ...
>
> Ideally, we would want to tax the net wealth of individuals. But such a tax is not easy to implement effectively. Estimating wealth accurately and fairly is a more complex exercise than estimating incomes. Further, many forms of wealth are mobile ... and can and will move.

Lawrence Wong cited the experience in the OECD countries where the number of countries that levy taxes on net wealth has dropped from 12

---

[19] Menon, *The Singapore Synthesis*, 93–94; Ramkishen S. Rajan and Bhavya Gupta, "Time to Consider a Wealth Tax for Singapore," *The Straits Times*, September 14, 2021, https://www.straitstimes.com/opinion/time-to-consider-a-wealth-tax-for-spore.

[20] Lawrence Wong, "Budget 2022 Speech — As Delivered," February 18, 2022, https://www.sgpc.gov.sg/sgpcmedia/media_releases/mof/press_release/P-20220218-3/attachment/Budget%202022%20Speech%20-%20As%20Delivered.pdf, 75.

in 1990 to only three in 2020, mainly because of implementation difficulties. He went on to say:

> *We will continue to study the experiences of other countries and explore options to tax wealth effectively. In the meantime, we will strengthen our current system of taxes.*

Clearly, the search for an effective wealth tax continues. While he did not introduce any new wealth taxes, he announced a hike in property taxes, which is currently the principal means of taxing wealth. A large detached house in the central area that is not owner-occupied will see an increase in the property tax bill to S$43,000 a year. For a similar owner-occupied property, the tax will go up to S$28,000 a year. These increases will be done in two steps.[21]

The question this raises is, will Singapore keep its policy of encouraging, and not dis-incentivising, wealth creation? I hope the answer is that it will.

In 2008, Tharman Shanmugaratnam, then Finance Minister, gave this explanation:

> *If we make Singapore an attractive place for wealth to be invested and built up, whether by Singaporeans or foreigners who bring their assets here, it will benefit our whole economy and society, not just the individuals who build up their wealth.*[22]

Philanthropy

I want to argue for another initiative — philanthropy. I feel strongly that philanthropy should be a key part of Singapore's desired future and build on the example set by our pioneer philanthropists. Rather than add more

---

[21] Ibid., 77.

[22] Tharman Shanmugaratnam, "Budget Statement 2008: Creating a Top Quality Economy, Building a Resilient Community," delivered in Parliament on February 15, 2008, https://www.mof.gov.sg/docs/default-source/default-document-library/singapore-budget/budget-archives/2008/fy2008_budget_statement.pdf?sfvrsn=cbc23f72_2, 23.

wealth taxes to address inequality, it might be more effective to promote and celebrate philanthropy on a wider scale. The aim should be to instil a sense of *noblesse oblige* among today's wealthy and encourage them to give back to our society.

Singapore has more than 400 foundations and trusts registered with the Commissioner of Charities (CoC). Of these, some 90 are large foundations that together gave out S$264 million in their latest financial year. They include the iconic Lee Foundation and Lien Foundation, as well as Temasek Foundation and the Community Foundation of Singapore.[23]

According to the CoC's 2020 annual report, the total charitable donations made in the financial Year of 2019 was S$3.25 billion, up 13 per cent, and it benefited some 2,300 registered charities.[24] A feasible desired future would be to double this by 2030 and aim for S$15–20 billion by 2045. This would be a significant component of our future society.

At a broader level, Singapore should also strive to be a society where everyone who can, helps others in need. The National Volunteer and Philanthropy Centre (NVPC), whose mission is to grow a culture of giving in Singapore, raised a record high of S$102 million in the Financial Year of 2020/2021 through Giving.sg, the national donation portal.[25] NVPC's role can be elevated, and bold new targets can also be set for donations by Singaporeans.

I recently attended the Singaporean of the Year awards organised by *ST*. All 10 nominees had remarkable stories. The one that made a big impression on me was a young couple who, during the COVID-19 pandemic, set up a "kindness corner" outside their Tampines flat where

---

[23] Theresa Tan, "Meet Singapore's Newer Philanthropic Foundations: They Give Millions, Seeking to Spark Social Change," *The Straits Times*, October 18, 2021, https://www.straitstimes.com/singapore/community/meet-spores-newer-philanthropic-foundations-they-give-millions-seeking-to-spark.

[24] Ministry of Culture, Community and Youth, "Commissioner of Charities Annual Report 2020," October 2021, https://www.charities.gov.sg/PublishingImages/Resource-and-Training/Publications/COC-Annual-Reports/Documents/Commissioner%20of%20Charities%20Annual%20Report%202020.pdf, 6–10.

[25] National Volunteer & Philanthropy Centre, "NVPC Celebrates the Generosity of Singapore with New Historic Milestone Surpassing $100M in Donations," April 13, 2021, https://cityofgood.sg/newsroom/nvpc-celebrates-the-generosity-of-singapore-with-new-historic-milestone-surpassing-100m-in-donations/.

those in need could pick up free groceries, no questions asked.[26] Imagine that. And imagine if many more Singaporeans were to emulate this and set up kindness corners all over Singapore's heartlands.

In fact, kindness should be made a part of our desired future, and the Singapore Kindness Movement can help get us there.

Happiness

Let me get back now to the pledge. My final comments are on the words "so as to achieve happiness". It was Rajaratnam who added the word "happiness", which the Cabinet retained.[27]

I remember the first time I had to recite the pledge in 1966 as a 12-year old. The word "happiness" jumped out at me. It felt like it did not quite belong, but I loved it. If there is one word we must never take out, it is happiness. God bless Rajaratnam.

But the question we can ask is, can we and should we do more to make happiness a key part of our desired future? My answer is, why not? What is the point of a desired future if happiness does not feature in it?

As far as I know, Bhutan is the only country that has made happiness part of state policy. It has a Gross National Happiness Index which, since 2008, has been part of the country's Constitution. But theirs is not the common meaning of happiness. It is a deeper, Buddhist notion. Their index measures the ingredients for happiness such as good health, well-being and a whole lot more; not whether people are happy in the usual joyful sense of the word.[28]

What Bhutan's experience tells us is that we do need to think about what our idea of happiness is or should be. In the meantime, however, there

---

[26] Syarafana Shafeeq, "ST Singaporean of the Year Nominee: Couple Offer Groceries to the Needy at Their Door," *The Straits Times*, November 1, 2021, https://www.straitstimes.com/singapore/couple-offer-groceries-to-the-needy-at-their-door.

[27] Wei and Saparudin, "National Pledge."

[28] University of Oxford, "Bhutan's Gross National Happiness Index," accessed May 9, 2022, https://ophi.org.uk/policy/gross-national-happiness-index.

is an urgent need to alleviate ill health, distress and discontent in our society. Woe betide us if this gets worse.

Let me summarise what I have said thus far:

1. The Singapore pledge forms an excellent basis for an updated desired future.
2. The goal of "one united people" should include other differences apart from race, language and religion.
3. We should add social mobility and inclusivity, in addition to equality.
4. We can leaven inequality of outcomes through philanthropy and kindness.
5. We should retain happiness as a goal, but define our idea of happiness.

New Areas in Desired Futures

The Climate Crisis and Sustainability

Let me move to new areas and issues that did not exist in 1966, which must feature in any new desired future. I will focus on three areas.

First, action on the climate crisis, and the broader challenge of sustainable development. I mentioned earlier Singapore's "net-zero" targets and the new carbon taxes. The climate crisis is without doubt *the* most urgent global challenge of our time.

Any desired future for Singapore must include the UN's broader Sustainable Development Goals (SDGs). The 17 SDGs were adopted by the UN in 2015.[29] Interestingly, an earlier UN policy document was titled "The Future We Want". I wish they had kept that name because, in effect, this is the UN's desired future for the world. There is no need for a further backcasting exercise here.

One success the UN has had is in mobilising the younger generation. The SDGs have caught the attention of the Millennials and Generation Z who worry that they will inherit a broken and degraded world. But what is

---

[29] United Nations, "The 17 Goals," accessed May 9, 2022, https://sdgs.un.org/goals.

needed are realistic pathways to the desired future — it cannot be reached by idealism alone.

Technology Advances and Artificial Intelligence

The next new area is technology advances. This is the hardest to both forecast and backcast. What we know is that the use and application of technologies, especially digital technologies, have seen high-speed advances in recent years. There have been sudden spurts just in the last five years in vehicle technology, for instance, from hybrid cars to fully electric cars and soon driverless cars.

Identifying which technologies will experience similar trends over the next two decades is made difficult by the cycle of hype and disillusionment that most emerging technologies go through. Yet, we must look over the horizon.

I do not propose to survey the whole field, but by all expert accounts, artificial intelligence (AI) merits special focus. Before we do any backcasting, we need to understand why AI is special:

1. AI involves smart machines that can perform tasks that typically require human intelligence. Indeed, this is technology of a unique kind.
   AI uses computers to harness massive amounts of data, then uses learned intelligence to make super-fast decisions, many times faster than humans. (In my last lecture, I spoke about real-time bidding in the digital advertising space. That's AI at work at the speed of light.)
2. AI will have a transformative impact on almost every industry.
3. Almost everyone agrees that AI's pervasive use is set to take off exponentially.

As if this is not enough, there are some kickers. Whereas AI-driven machines and robots have so far been deployed for lower-value, repetitive work, in the future it will affect high-value intellectual tasks, in almost all professions — medicine, accounting, law, and the list goes on. The productivity gains will be huge, but many higher-end jobs will be at risk.[30]

A further factor is the geopolitical contest in technology. This will be an added spur that will drive technology at speeds not seen before. We need only look at the speed at which COVID-19 vaccines were developed. One worry, however, is the development of AI in harmful directions.

If we backcast to the present, the best strategy is to embrace AI fully. Being short of labour, we can reduce our reliance on Singapore-based foreign manpower through AI's productivity gains.

But we will have to figure out how to deal with two challenges:

1. Ensuring we have the AI skills to drive an AI economy, and finding ways to tap remote skills using our global connectivity.
2. Being prepared to manage big spikes in job displacements and having in place retraining and re-skilling schemes.

How best can all of this be captured in Singapore's desired future? I would describe this dimension's desired future for Singapore this way:

An AI-driven economy and society, where we enjoy the full productivity dividends through our global connectivity but effectively address the threat of job displacements.

The Internet and the Metaverse

I move now to the Internet and the metaverse. I spoke in my last lecture on how achieving a global consensus on governance of the Internet will be a bridge too far, and Singapore will have to find its way forward.

I also outlined a desired future for the Internet — a secure, trustworthy, inclusive and open system. If we backcast to what steps we need now, each of those goals requires collaborative action:

1. To be secure, we will have to deal with scams, fraud and cybercrime. We would also have to look at how to keep it safe for children especially.

---

[30] Jennifer Liu, "High-Paid, Well-Educated White Collar Workers Will Be Heavily Affected by AI, Says New Report," *CNBC*, November 27, 2019, https://www.cnbc.com/2019/11/27/high-paid-well-educated-white-collar-jobs-heavily-affected-by-ai-new-report.html.

2. To be trustworthy, effective ways must be found to deal with fake news, wilful misinformation and outright propaganda.
3. To be inclusive, we will require steps to deal with society's digital divide.
4. To remain open, we will have to successfully keep the Internet safe and keep out crooks and criminals.

Let me speak next about the metaverse. For sure, it will be part of the future. There is a good reason why Facebook took the bold step of rebranding its parent company, Meta.

I recently read a report on the top 100 trends produced yearly by a consultancy called Wunderman Thompson. Of the top 100 trends for 2022, seven were related to the metaverse. Let me quote from the Wunderman Thompson report, titled "The Future 100: 2022":

> *A new digital era is on the horizon as the metaverse evolves from a sci-fi concept into a reality. Virtual worlds, where people can gather, create, buy and sell, socialise, live and work, are becoming the new hangouts.*[31]

It goes on to talk of advanced avatars, virtual teleportation, marketplaces for non-fungible tokens (NFTs) and a new direct-to-avatar retail model.

All of this might sound like science fiction, but parts of the metaverse are already here. I mentioned in my previous lecture sites like Roblox, which already have a huge teenage audience. Coincidentally, soon after I mentioned it, a teenage girl in the US was kidnapped and sexually abused by an older man she met on Roblox.[32] Clearly, there are dangers too.

For Singapore's desired future, our best option on the metaverse is simply to accept its existence, be a part of it and benefit from its opportunities.

To get there, we need to be closely engaged with the metaverse from here. We should do it if only because our young will be deeply in it. We will also need to take steps to keep it safe and keep out the bad actors.

---

[31] Emma Chiu, and Wunderman Thompson, "Foreword," *The Future 100: Trends and Change to Watch in 2022*, accessed May 9, 2022, https://www.wundermanthompson.com/insight/the-future-100-2022.

[32] "Young Girl Returned after Kidnapping by Man She Met on Roblox," *BBC*, March 3, 2022, https://www.bbc.com/news/world-us-canada-60607782.

Keeping Singapore Going

Let me summarise the action needed in the new areas I have covered:

1. Act on the climate crisis and adopt the UN's 17 SDGs.
2. Embrace AI, seize the productivity gains but prepare for job displacements.
3. Work towards a secure, trustworthy, inclusive and open Internet.
4. Be closely engaged with the metaverse.

This is by no means an exhaustive list. Together with my earlier list of updates to the Singapore pledge, they will keep Singapore going to 2045, one milestone at a time.

There are some areas that I have not been able to cover:

1. The fundamentals, such as good governance with no corruption, meritocracy, resilience, remaining open and global, and ensuring a competitive economy that produces good jobs as well as good returns.
2. Shared core values, such as hard work, integrity, tolerance and kindness.

Taking in all these, the overall desired future for Singapore is:

A well-governed, peaceful, safe and thriving city-state, concerned about sustainability of our planet, abiding by its core values, and where its people are united, inclusive, socially mobile, kind and happy (in the full sense of the word).

This concludes my views on desired futures for Singapore. With this as the broad backdrop, I will now talk about desired futures for the Singapore media.

Desired Futures for the Singapore Media

The local legacy media will of course have a big role to play in Singapore's desired futures and in getting there. But they must first keep themselves going, have their own desired future and plot their own path. I will cover this now in the last part of my lecture.

I will again focus my comments on the future of the legacy media, in particular the SPH Media Trust (SMT). Also, I am speaking in my personal capacity, so these are my own views.

I explained in my first lecture the background and rationale for the creation of SMT. Parliament has just approved the funding support for SMT, of S$180 million for Financial Year 2022 starting 1 April 2022. The government has said it will provide this annual funding for an initial five-year period, if annual targets are met.[33]

Envisioning 2045

Let me deal first with the future of journalism in Singapore, and then look at the future of SMT. I am going to transport myself to 2045 and describe what a feasible desired future for local journalism would look like:

1. There are good audiences in English and Mandarin for high-quality, trusted news content, both in written and audio-visual forms. For Malay and Tamil news media, there are smaller but loyal audiences.
2. Niche content on other topics (everything from politics to food) also have decent audiences.
3. Content is of course delivered largely in digital formats. The print format is delivered as e-papers on tablets and other digital devices.
4. There are more players in local journalism than before, mostly in niche spaces.
5. There are myriad other sources of news all over the Web.

With that journalism backdrop, let me next describe a feasible future for SMT. Remember, I am still in 2045:

1. SMT distinguishes its offerings from others through the quality of its content. However, the key differentiator is the trust it has gained from users over the years through accurate and balanced coverage.
2. Strong SMT newsrooms, well supported by technology and AI, produce compelling content.

---

[33] Goh Yan Han, "SPH Media Trust to Get up to $180m a Year in Government Funding for Next Five Years," *The Straits Times*, March 4, 2022, https://www.straitstimes.com/singapore/politics/sph-media-trust-to-get-up-to-180m-a-year-in-government-funding-for-next-five-years.

3. SMT's regional and international paid reach has grown, after years of strong subscription campaigns.
4. *Lianhe Zaobao* has wide reach both in China and among the Chinese diaspora outside China.
5. SMT's Malay and Tamil papers, having invested in stronger newsrooms, are alive and well, supported partly by benefactors.

If you were to ask me to summarise what I have said and describe the future SMT in one sentence, here is what I will say:

A financially independent, thriving media group whose products in four languages are trusted by both their Singapore audience and regional and international audiences, all of whom pay for their premium content.

You will have noticed I said the SMT is financially independent in the future. I will come back to that shortly.

What It Will Take to Get There

Backcasting to today, what will it take for SMT to get to its desired future? I will list six priorities:

1. Forward-looking people policies, with a sharp focus on talent acquisition and retention, and on high employee engagement.
2. Continuous investments in the technology stack to support journalists and news operations, as well as all other functions, with greater use of data and AI to drive innovations.
3. Capability in subscription sales for both corporate sales and international sales, and more attention paid to satisfying customers.
4. A sustained effort is to turn around the long decline in advertising revenues, through new strategies that capitalise on SMT's current total reach of 73 per cent, supported by the use of technology.[34]

---

[34] Singapore Press Holdings, "7 in 10 of Singapore Population Access SPH Content Properties Weekly, SPH Number 1 in Digital News: GfK Research," September 2, 2021, https://www.imsph.sg/7-in-10-of-singapore-population-access-sph-content-properties-weekly-sph-number-1-in-digital-news-gfk-research/.

5. Targeted investments in media-related businesses to generate new streams of future revenue.
6. Broad community support for its mission of providing trusted news, in four languages, as a public good.

Given the resources, I am confident SMT's strategies will succeed. This is why I believe it is feasible for SMT to achieve its medium-term goal of being financially independent.

Why I Am Confident

Let me conclude by giving you results from two recent surveys. They show strong interest in news and readership and high levels of trust in Singapore. I believe SMT can build on this and grow.

Figure 1.   Reasons for Internet Use (%)

"How often do you connect to the Internet for_____?"
Percentage of those who said Often or Very Often.

	December 2020	July 2021	December 2021
Monetary transactions	61.4	63.9	62.1
Stay informed of latest news	76.3	78.0	81.3
Conduct search using search engines	77.8	80.6	78.0
Find information on directions or for transport	62.1	66.3	61.1
For work or school	70.0	68.9	74.5
Access cloud storage	44.0	42.6	42.4
For entertainment	65.1	68.9	72.6
Access government services	51.8	50.6	49.4
Connect with friends and loved ones	67.9	67.2	67.4

Source: Edson C. Tandoc, Goh Zhang Hao and Edmund W. J. Lee, Centre for Information Integrity and the Internet (IN-cube), IN-cube Working Paper No.1, "Digital Life During a Pandemic: Results from a Panel Study," 2022.

Figure 2. Singapore News Outlets Brand Trust Scores

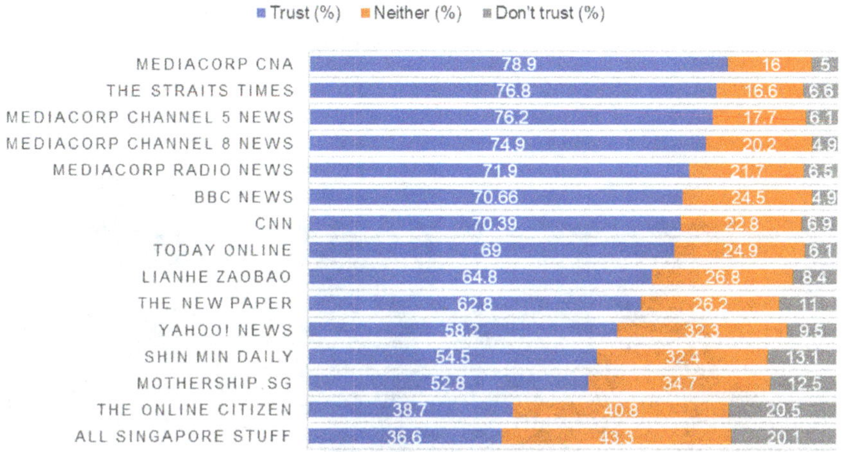

■ Trust (%)   ■ Neither (%)   ■ Don't trust (%)

Outlet	Trust (%)	Neither (%)	Don't trust (%)
MEDIACORP CNA	78.9	16	5
THE STRAITS TIMES	76.8	16.6	6.6
MEDIACORP CHANNEL 5 NEWS	76.2	17.7	6.1
MEDIACORP CHANNEL 8 NEWS	74.9	20.2	4.9
MEDIACORP RADIO NEWS	71.9	21.7	6.5
BBC NEWS	70.66	24.5	4.9
CNN	70.39	22.8	6.9
TODAY ONLINE	69	24.9	6.1
LIANHE ZAOBAO	64.8	26.8	8.4
THE NEW PAPER	62.8	26.2	11
YAHOO! NEWS	58.2	32.3	9.5
SHIN MIN DAILY	54.5	32.4	13.1
MOTHERSHIP SG	52.8	34.7	12.5
THE ONLINE CITIZEN	38.7	40.8	20.5
ALL SINGAPORE STUFF	36.6	43.3	20.1

Source: Reuters Institute for the Study of Journalism and University of Oxford, Digital News Report 2021, Singapore, "Brand Trust Scores," accessed May 13, 2022, https://reutersinstitute.politics.ox.ac.uk/digital-news-report/2021/singapore.

Thank you very much, ladies and gentlemen. I have enjoyed doing the three lectures. I hope you have found them useful.

Question-and-Answer Session
Moderated by Dr Shashi Jayakumar

Mr Patrick Daniel speaking with Dr Shashi Jayakumar at the Q&A session
Source: Jacky Ho for the Institute of Policy Studies

Dr Shashi Jayakumar: Thanks to the audience members who have come and agreed to listen to what Patrick had to say today. There is plenty of food for thought in what he has given us. In what follows, I will also try to bring in what has been said so thought provokingly across the first two lectures.

Patrick, I am very impressed by your backcasting methodology, but I am a bit of an old fogey myself, so I do not have access to this kind of advanced, futuristic thinking. So, if I may, allow me to do the old-fashioned method of "future casting". You try to sketch out what the best outcomes are in many spheres of our society in 2045 — mainstream society, the youth, as well as the SMT. If I could also play the devil's advocate and suggest that in the future some of the things you are positing may not work out quite as well as you hope.

When I engage with young people in my research, I always ask them what platforms or news sources they engage with. Quite often the most popular answers might be platforms like TikTok (especially over the last few years) as well as WhatsApp and Instagram. And believe it or not, as counter-intuitive as it may seem, we may have to accept that they are getting news from sources that are not primarily (from our vantage point) news sources. Their communications platforms change and flow. If I asked them three years ago, they may have said Snapchat instead. I am trying to parlay all of this into a question, so bear with me.

In this desired future in 2045, SMT and its offerings want to have a stable base where the youth of today — the future backbone of Singapore's middle-class society in the future — trust it, regularly resort to it, and find it credible and trustworthy. Here are a couple of questions where I would appreciate your thoughts. When SMT gets to that future where it is regularly read and listened to, to what degree should it be imitative of some of the other technologies I have been talking about? For example, using the methodology of TikTok videos, and other things that some of us might find even a little bit gimmicky that are used by new media platforms. Furthermore, to what degree, if it chooses to go into that kind of future, would this possibly lead to a shallowing of discourse? The final question is: Although we want SMT's offerings in the future to be trusted, respected and credible, is there a risk that it may be all those things but also become rather a niche and highbrow? Could it morph into a resource for the educated and the real intelligentsia or the administrators of Singapore? I appreciate that this was a mishmash of questions, but feel free to elaborate.

Mr Patrick Daniel: The first thing I will say is that these are things that we track quite closely. For example, I know that the common view is that we are losing young readers. Actually, I am aware that the government has non-public data showing that even from the ages of 15 to 24, our readership is quite high. It is also high for ages 25 to 34.

Of course, it all depends on which surveys you look at. The latest data that were just sent to me was that the readership of *The Straits Times* actually mirrors the profile of Singapore. So, Generation Z, aged 15 to 24, comprises 13 per cent of Singaporeans aged 15 and above. *The Straits Times'* readership by that group is 12 per cent. Then take Millennials, which comprise 29 per cent of the national profile. Readership of *The Straits Times* by this group is at exactly 29 per cent. Generation X, who are aged 40 to 54 now, make up 25 per cent of our national profile. Readership for *The Straits Times* by this generation is at 30 per cent of total readers. Interestingly, beyond this age group, the older generation's readership numbers are not as high because much of our content is all digital. So, when you get to the older group, you find that the numbers drop.

There are two points I want to make. Number one is — and this is so critical to us — if by 2045 we have lost all the youths, there won't be anybody reading us. So, we know that and therefore we are tracking it closely.

My second point is that the numbers actually look quite positive, not just in this survey, but across several other surveys as well. Everybody is checking the age groups of readership — including how long each group reads and where they read. The difference is that the youths are reading a variety of news sources, while the older generation just reads legacy newspapers including foreign news sources.

I have a third point. We have followed youths across all technology platforms — you name it, we are there. However, we are small. We do not yet have mass readership on these platforms, we are just experimenting and seeing what people like. We have not invested huge amounts of money on all these platforms but we are there. Very early on, we went into YouTube and put up free content. My former colleagues took the step to go onto these platforms and I am encouraged by the numbers. So, whether you backcast or forecast, I think that there is a feasible future for SMT's papers to be well-read in 2045.

The second part of your question is the shallowing of intellectual discourse. If you are in the news business, there are two choices. You could forget about the old-fashioned ways and just go after what the kids are doing because they are the future. So, if they are going to TikTok, you move to TikTok and forget the core business. We have not done that. So that part of the business, the news business from the legacy media, will remain the core. We are on these platforms to experiment and see what works for us so that we know what to do next. So, I would not worry so much about the shallowing of discourse.

You will actually be very surprised at the number of things that Singaporeans read in the newspapers. It staggers visitors who come here. I recall one French journalist who came here in the middle of their presidential election and he was surprised by the amount of space we gave to it. Everywhere he went, people were following the election and asked him who was going to win. So actually, Singaporeans are quite well informed.

Having said that, I would say one problem is the amount of misinformation that occurs on platforms like Twitter and WhatsApp. I get them all the time. You do not know what to believe anymore. I do wonder how we will deal with this. Fake news is coming from all over the place. I wonder whether it will be enough just to focus on quality content and trustworthiness, while in the meantime, social media is buzzing with all kinds of falsehoods. I have to say that I don't quite know yet how best to deal with this aspect.

Dr Jayakumar: It is a long answer, but a good answer. I am a national security researcher and you are a seasoned media practitioner. I am not sure about you but for my line of work, this calls for almost eternal pessimism looking at some of these things you have just alluded to — contemporary issues that have to do with security, but which cut to the heart of national discourse and resilience as well.

I am personally, and from the point of view of my centre (Centre of Excellence for National Security), increasingly concerned that while top-level decision-makers might make calls based on very good grounds — like national security principles and international law, for example — quite often the discourse — and this is heavily anecdotal of course — may well be at the coffee shop level. People are asking, "Why do we do this? Why do we behave this way? Do we really need to get our necks stuck into all these issues?" I am sure you are familiar with these questions, but I am not talking about any one particular flash point, because this could apply to many things.

Hold that thought if you will, and let us get back to 2045 and the SMT stable's offerings. I am not going to fill in the words for you, but SMT certainly has a role in conveying the news in an impartial, factual yet analytical fashion. If it expands on this, should it additionally play some role in terms of national discourse? Should the media play some sort of role beyond reporting the factual and analytical in terms of putting us roughly on some plane of national discourse where we may agree to disagree? Could it be a platform for us to talk intelligently and rationally where we are not splintered aside by polarisations of thought?

Mr Daniel: It is a tough challenge you are posing, but I would say that we first need to get the basics right, which is to put out accurate stories and stick to what is factual. Of course, we also want to discuss intelligently, rationally and reasonably about national issues.

The challenge is where there is polarisation of thought. Where messages or stories are actually debunked, how far do we go to clearly state that they have been debunked, because these stories keep coming up again? Not that we should go out of our way to debunk people, but where we know that something is not true, we should contribute to that conversation in a better way. Even then, it is still very difficult. If you look at current affairs, the spin is now coming even from official spokesmen. You go to a press conference and the official spokesman says something and you question whether this information is factual. Do you report it or not, even if the spokesman is lying through his teeth? So, this is uncharted. This applies to all sides, regardless of political leaning. So, it becomes very difficult for us news outlets to hold the ground and lift ourselves a bit higher out of the mud. I have been in the business for 30 years and I have not seen such unprecedented amounts of factual latitude. People just invent their stories and their facts.

This could just be a crazy phase. However, it has gotten to a point now where there is confirmation bias and all manner of other biases. I spoke about this in my last lecture as well. People read a story and they hate it because it does not accord with their worldview. So, it is very hard for us to balance this. Do we just go straight down the middle and let the people who disagree fall off and stop reading? It is going to be a challenge so I do not have the best answer for you.

Dr Jayakumar: Just to press you a little bit, in your first lecture you talked about the history of *The Straits Times* and other newspapers under SPH. You were very clear that the policymakers and media leaders here historically had a view of the media which was different from what was seen in the West — that the media is not a fourth estate; it does not stand for crusading journalism and does not exist primarily to call out or to check on the powers of the executive.

Could you comment on the overall tone and tenor of SMT's role in the national narrative? From the policymakers' point of view, it would be ideal if you had a stable of offerings that supported this issue of cohesion, and I strongly expect that cohesion is increasingly going to be under stress in the decades to come. However, this is perhaps how the policymakers might feel. So what about from the reporters' point of view? This is especially if SMT's offerings might want other things as well. For example, to bring in eyeballs or to compete with technologically infused offerings. Would you have any thoughts on that?

Mr Daniel: Your last point is key. The one thing we must not do is chase after eyeballs. Look at where that has led social media sites. I will not mention names but look at the giant tech companies and where this has led them. Why? Because they are all chasing eyeballs. If something on social media makes you angry, the site sends you more content to make you even angrier. That kind of approach is just going to lead you down into the back alleys and the rubbish bins. That we will not do. We will not chase eyeballs. If you think you are old, we are old too; and we want to do traditional journalism. We are not going to chase after people or spill as much dirt as we can. That is not the role that we want to play, because your batting average is actually very low and you get it wrong half the time.

Unfortunately, we cannot help you with national security and resilience very much, but we can be the purveyor of accurate news. If we can do that and people read it, that is the important part. But if we do not have readers then we are of no use. So, our stories have to be compelling, they have got to be right on the button and accurate and people have to trust them. We must make sure that we report truthfully and that we check what we report.

Dr Jayakumar: I would like to take some of the audience's questions now, and one of the more interesting ones concerns how AI will impact journalism. The question is actually quite a blunt one: Will journalism become obsolete? What should journalists do to remain relevant? Patrick, we have had past discussions on how there has actually been pretty passable journalism written not by humans but by algorithms. You had time to go into some of this in your lecture, but would you care to expand on this?

Mr Daniel: The word you use is an important one. AI journalism is passable. We could put DBS' financial results through AI and the algorithm would produce a passable story. It will get all the facts and numbers right, but we have to go beyond passable. For companies as big as DBS, I would want a seasoned journalist to write it. We might put some smaller companies through AI because we don't have enough journalists to write them all up. If AI can help us to do those stories, why not? AI is already being used for recommendation engines. If you want to track personalised news choices, AI will do it for you. But I do not think journalists are going to be redundant.

We still need good journalists with judgement, and AI does not have the editor's judgement as yet.

Dr Jayakumar: Thank you, Patrick. I take heart from that because presumably, if you are saying that about the business journalism space, for the writing of national security reports, that day is even further away. Looking at the audience questions, as well as how much more we still need to cover — I wish we had more time — maybe I will ask one or two final questions.

You have highlighted in this lecture and touched on in the past lectures, the role of the young — heart-warming examples of how the young come together in creative, innovative and ingenious ways to help. In my own research, this is what I find as well. People accuse them of being snowflakes and strawberries. We know what it means, but it is not really borne out in what I see. I would be interested to hear what you have to say either in your journalistic work or just your general experiences with youths, because they are the future backbone of society and the core of your future readership. What heart or lack thereof do you take from your sense of them?

Mr Daniel: Let me start with my kids. When my daughter who is now 30 did her A-Level General Paper (GP) examination, I asked her what GP essay topic she chose. She chose this topic: If you are a celebrity, are you entitled to privacy? When she told me what she had written, I was impressed, because she does not touch the print newspapers at home and yet is obviously on top of the news. I find that most young people are actually quite well informed. Where they get the news from, I have not figured out yet. But they are very well informed and this is good for us.

My second point is that youths go through life cycles of their own. What they did when they were 18 is different from what they will do when they are 30, and that is different from what they do when they have kids. I feel that we should not look at it in a linear way, and we should actually see how people live their lives. That is why I am hopeful that if we keep to our core role and don't go chasing eyeballs, people will come to us and read us. During the pandemic, it was clear that if readers wanted to know about COVID-19 and what the latest policy is, they would come to us. The numbers show that when readers want accurate news, they come to us.

Dr Jayakumar: Thank you very much, Patrick. I sincerely wish we had time for more, maybe a fourth lecture? You have really enlivened us and indeed not just in this lecture, but your first two as well, which we all followed. They have given us a lot of texture, and they were hopeful and uplifting for the future, not just for the media landscape but for the future of our society and our young too.

Bibliography

Alphabet Inc. "Alphabet Annual Report 2021." Accessed April 25, 2022. https://abc.xyz/investor/static/pdf/20220202_alphabet_10K.pdf?cache=fc81690.

Alphabet Inc. "Revenue Recognition." Alphabet Annual Report 2021. Accessed April 15, 2022. https://abc.xyz/investor/static/pdf/20220202_alphabet_10K.pdf.

Balakrishnan, Vivian. "Edited Transcript of Opening Address by Minister for Foreign Affairs Dr Vivian Balakrishnan at the 10th Asia-Pacific Programme for Senior National Security Officers on April 11, 2016, 9am at the Marina Mandarin." *Ministry of Foreign Affairs*. https://www.mfa.gov.sg/Newsroom/Press-Statements-Transcripts-and-Photos/2016/04/Edited-Transcript-of-Opening-Address-by-Minister-for-Foreign-Affairs-Dr-Vivian-Balakrishnan-at-the-1.

Belson, Ken. "EBay to Buy Skype, Internet Phone Service for $2.6 billion." *The New York Times*, September 13, 2005. https://www.nytimes.com/2005/09/13/technology/ebay-to-buy-skype-internet-phone-service-for-26-billion.html.

Bhaumik, Subir. "Why Did Muslim Hardliners Attack Hindus in Bangladesh's Worst Bout of Communal Violence in Two Decades?" *South China Morning Post*, October 20, 2021. https://www.scmp.com/week-asia/politics/article/3153016/why-did-muslims-attack-hindus-bangladeshs-worst-bout-communal.

Carlyle, Thomas. *On Heroes, Hero-Worship and the Heroic in History: Six Lectures*. London: J. Fraser, 1841.

Carlyle, Thomas. "The Fourth Estate." In *The Works of Thomas Carlyle: The French Revolution: A History | Volume 2*, edited by Henry Duff Traill, 235. Cambridge: Cambridge University Press, 2010.

Centre for International Governance Innovation and Chatham House. "Preface." In *Global Commission on Internet Governance: One Internet*, 9–10. CIGI and Chatham House, 2016. https://www.cigionline.org/static/documents/gcig_final_report_-_with_cover.pdf.

Cheong Yip Seng. *OB Markers: My Straits Times Story*. Singapore: Straits Times Press, 2013.

Chia, Joshua Yeong Jia and Nor-Afidah Abd Rahman. "Utusan Melayu." *Singapore Infopedia*, 2016. https://eresources.nlb.gov.sg/infopedia/articles/SIP_1088_2007-06-12.html.

Chiu, Emma. Wunderman Thompson. "Foreword." *The Future 100: Trends and Change to Watch in 2022*. Accessed May 9, 2022. https://www.wundermanthompson.com/insight/the-future-100-2022.

"Constitution of the Republic of Singapore." Singapore Statutes Online Accessed April 14, 2022. https://sso.agc.gov.sg/Act/CONS1963?ProvIds=pr14-.

Cramer-Flood, Ethan. "Worldwide Digital Ad Spending 2021." *eMarketer*, April 29, 2021. https://www.emarketer.com/content/worldwide-digital-ad-spending-2021.

DataReportal. "Digital 2022: Global Overview Report." January 26, 2022. https://datareportal.com/reports/digital-2022-global-overview-report.

Defense Advanced research Projects Agency (DARPA). "DARPA. 60 Years: 1958–2018." Accessed August 25, 2022. https://www.darpa.mil/attachments/DARAPA60_publication-no-ads.pdf, 4.

European Court of Human Rights, Council of Europe. "European Convention on Human Rights." Accessed April 14, 2022. https://www.echr.coe.int/documents/convention_eng.pdf.

Feiner, Lauren. "Facebook Stock Plummets 26% in its Biggest One-Day Drop Ever." *CNBC*, February 3, 2022. https://www.cnbc.com/2022/02/03/facebook-shares-plummet-22percent-after-reporting-weak-guidance.html.

"First Amendment." Constitution of the United States. Accessed April 14, 2022. https://constitution.congress.gov/constitution/amendment-1/#amendment-1.

Foley, Simon. *Understanding Media Propaganda in the 21st Century: Manufacturing Consent Revisited and Revised*. Cambridge: Cambridge Scholars Publishing, 2021.

Fukuyama, Francis. Putin's War on the Liberal Order. *The Straits Times,* March 9, 2022. https://www.straitstimes.com/opinion/putins-war-on-the-liberal-order.

Fukuyama, Francis, Barak Richman, and Ashish Goel. "How to Save Democracy From Technology." *Foreign Affairs*, January/February 2021. https://www.foreignaffairs.com/articles/united-states/2020-11-24/fukuyama-how-save-democracy-technology?check_logged_in=1&utm_medium=promo_email&utm_source=lo_flows&utm_campaign=registered_user_welcome&utm_term=email_1&utm_content=20220422.

Goh, Yan Han. "SPH Media Trust to Get Up to $180m a Year in Government Funding for Next Five Years." *The Straits Times,* March 4, 2022. https://www.straitstimes.com/singapore/politics/sph-media-trust-to-get-up-to-180m-a-year-in-government-funding-for-next-five-years.

"Google buys YouTube for $1.65 billion." *NBC News*, October 9, 2006. https://www.nbcnews.com/id/wbna15196982.

Government of France. "The Declaration of the Rights of Man and of the Citizen." Accessed April 14, 2022. https://www.elysee.fr/en/french-presidency/the-declaration-of-the-rights-of-man-and-of-the-citizen.

Government of Singapore. "Newspaper and Printing Presses Act 1974." Singapore Statuses Online. Accessed April 14, 2022. https://sso.agc.gov.sg/Act/NPPA1974?ProvIds=P11-#pr1-.

Government of Singapore. "Newspaper and Printing Presses (Amendment) Act 1986." Singapore Statuses Online. Accessed April 14, 2022. https://sso.agc.gov.sg/Acts-Supp/22-1986/Published/19860830?DocDate=19860830.

Hamilton, Walter. "Nasdaq's Stunning Rise Carried Index Past 5,000." *Los Angeles Times*, March 10, 2000. https://www.latimes.com/archives/la-xpm-2000-mar-10-mn-7290-story.html.

HistorySG. "Formation of Singapore Press Holdings." 2014. https://eresources.nlb.gov.sg/history/events/34789177-5f5e-468d-9a77-db3680ce4161.

Ho, Grace. "The Straits Times Remains Best-read Title, With Clear Shift to Digital, Across All Age Groups: Survey." *The Straits Times*, September 20, 2021. https://www.straitstimes.com/singapore/community/the-straits-times-remains-best-read-title-with-clear-shift-to-digital-across-all.

Hwang, Tim. *Subprime Attention Crisis: Advertising and the Time Bomb at the Heart of the Internet*. New York: Farrar, Straus and Giroux, 2020.

International Labour Organization. "Sub-minimum Wages for Migrant Workers." Accessed May 6, 2022. https://www.ilo.org/global/topics/wages/minimum-wages/rates/WCMS_451251/lang--en/index.htm

International Telecommunication Union. "Individuals Using the Internet." [2005–2021 data]. Accessed April 22, 2022. https://www.itu.int/en/ITU-D/Statistics/Pages/stat/default.aspx.

"Key milestones in the development of Internet". *The Sydney Morning Herald*, August 31, 2009. https://www.smh.com.au/technology/key-milestones-in-the-development-of-internet-20090831-f43x.html.

Kosseff, Jeff. *The Twenty-Six Words That Created the Internet*. New York: Cornell University Press, 2019.

Lee, Hsien Loong. "National Day Rally 2021." August 29, 2021. https://www.pmo.gov.sg/Newsroom/National-Day-Rally-2021-English.

Lee, Kuan Yew. "Address to the General Assembly of the International Press Institute at Helsinki Wednesday, 9th June 1971." *National Archives of Singapore*, Accessed April 14, 2022. https://www.nas.gov.sg/archivesonline/data/pdfdoc/lky19710609a.pdf.

Lee, Kuan Yew. *From Third World to First*. New York: HarperCollins, 2000.

Lee, Kuan Yew. "Mr. Lee Kuan Yew Replies to the Straits Times." *The Straits Times*, May 22, 1959.

Lee, Mei Yu. "Sin Chew Jit Poh." *Singapore Infopedia*, 2020. https://eresources.nlb.gov.sg/infopedia/articles/SIP_2021-04-05_145051.html.

Lent, John A. "Restructuring of Mass Media in Malaysia and Singapore — Pounding in the Coffin Nails?" *Bulletin of Concerned Asian Scholars* 16, no. 4 (1984): 26–35.

Leow, Annabeth. "Decisive Net-Zero Shift Will Establish Singapore's Economic Chops: Teo Chee Hean." *The Business Times,* March 9, 2022. https://www.businesstimes.com.sg/government-economy/decisive-net-zero-shift-will-establish-singapores-economic-chops-teo-chee-hean-0.

Liu, Jennifer. "High-Paid, Well-Educated White Collar Workers Will Be Heavily Affected by AI, Says New Report." *CNBC,* November 27, 2019. https://www.cnbc.com/2019/11/27/high-paid-well-educated-white-collar-jobs-heavily-affected-by-ai-new-report.html.

Mackintosh, Eliza. "Facebook Knew It was Being Used to Incite Violence in Ethiopia. It Did Little to Stop the Spread, Documents Show." *CNN*, October 25, 2021. https://edition.cnn.com/2021/10/25/business/ethiopia-violence-facebook-papers-cmd-intl/index.html.

Macleod, Christopher. "John Stuart Mill." In *The Stanford Encyclopedia of Philosophy,* Summer 2020 Edition.

Marketing Charts. "Most Negative Aspects of Programmatic Ad Buying." July 2018. https://www.marketingcharts.com/charts/negative-aspects-programmatic-ad-buying.

Mathew, Mathews, Leonard Lim, and Shanthini Selvarajan. "Religion, Morality and Conservatism in Singapore." IPS Working Papers No 34 (May 2019): 62–63.

Menon, Ravi. *The Singapore Synthesis: Innovation, Inclusion, Inspiration*. Singapore: World Scientific Publishing, 2022.

Meta Investor Relations. "Facebook Reports Fourth Quarter and Full Year 2021 Results." February 2, 2022. https://investor.fb.com/investor-news/press-release-details/2022/Meta-Reports-Fourth-Quarter-and-Full-Year-2021-Results/default.aspx.

Meta Platforms Inc. "Revenue." Meta Annual Report 2021. Accessed April 15, 2022. https://d18rn0p25nwr6d.cloudfront.net/CIK-0001326801/14039b47-2e2f-4054-9dc5-71bcc7cf01ce.pdf.

Mill, John Stuart. *On Liberty*. 1859; reissue. Canada: Batoche Books, 2001.

Ministry of Culture, Community and Youth. "Commissioner of Charities Annual Report 2020." October 2021, https://www.charities.gov.sg/PublishingImages/Resource-and-Training/Publications/COC-Annual-Reports/Documents/Commissioner%20of%20Charities%20Annual%20Report%202020.pdf.

Ministry of Manpower. "Factsheet — Workfare Income Supplement." 2010. https://www.mom.gov.sg/-/media/mom/documents/speeches/2010/factsheet---wis-(110310).pdf.

Ministry of Manpower. "Foreign Workforce Numbers." Accessed March 16, 2022. https://www.mom.gov.sg/documents-and-publications/foreign-workforce-numbers.

Ministry of Manpower, Manpower Research & Statistics Department. Resident Labour Force Aged Fifteen Years and Over by Highest Qualification Attained and Sex, 2011–2021 (June). January 28, 2022. https://stats.mom.gov.sg/iMAS_Tables1/LabourForce/LabourForce_2021/mrsd_2021LabourForce_T8.xlsx.

Ministry of Trade and Industry. "Feature Article: The Impact of the Workfare Income Supplement Scheme on Individuals' Labour Outcome." August 12, 2014. https://www.mti.gov.sg/-/media/MTI/Legislation/Public-Consultations/2014/The-Impact-Of-The-Workfare-Income-Supplement-Scheme-on-Individuals-Labour-Outcomes/fa_2q14.pdf?la=en&hash=A04FA8D339AD599621D8ADE1AE06BAF3.

"Mr Lee Eu Seng Released from Detention." Ministry of Home Affairs Press Release. National Archives Singapore, 1978. Accessed April 15, 2022. https://www.nas.gov.sg/archivesonline/data/pdfdoc/785-1978-02-01.pdf.

Nathan, S. R. *An Unexpected Journey: Path to the Presidency*. Singapore: Editions Didier Millet Pte Ltd, 2011.

National Heritage Board. "National Pledge." Accessed May 6, 2022. https://www.nhb.gov.sg/what-we-do/our-work/community-engagement/education/resources/national-symbols/national-pledge.

Ong, Justin. "SPH Media Trust Has Exercised Editorial Independence, This Will Not Change With Govt Funding: Josephine Teo." *The Straits Times,* February 15, 2022. https://www.straitstimes.com/singapore/politics/sph-media-trust-has-exercised-editorial-independence-this-will-not-change-with-government-funding-josephine-teo.

Perrin, Nicole. "Why Our Forecast of 2021 US Programmatic Digital Ad Spending is Now $15 Billion Higher." *eMarketer,* June 30, 2021. https://www.emarketer.com/content/forecast-2021-us-programmatic-digital-display-ad-spending-15-billion-higher.

Pew Research Center, Newspapers Fact Sheet. "Estimated Advertising and Circulation Revenue of the Newspaper Industry." June 29, 2021. https://www.pewresearch.org/journalism/fact-sheet/newspapers/.

Rajan, Ramkishen S. and Bhavya Gupta. "Time To Consider A Wealth Tax For Singapore." *The Straits Times,* September 14, 2021. https://www.straitstimes.com/opinion/time-to-consider-a-wealth-tax-for-spore.

Rekhi, Shefali. "ST Turns 175: Previous Editors on the Paper's Place in Society." *The Straits Times,* July 15, 2020. https://www.straitstimes.com/singapore/st175-previous-editors-on-st.

Reporters Without Borders. "Detailed Methodology." Accessed September 1, 2022. https://rsf.org/en/index-methodologie-2013-21.

Reporters Without Borders. "Index Details: Data of Press Freedom Ranking 2021." Accessed April 14, 2022. https://rsf.org/en/ranking_table.

Reporters Without Borders. "RSF Explains Why Singapore's Anti-fake News Bill is Terrible." April 8, 2019. https://rsf.org/en/news/rsf-explains-why-singapores-anti-fake-news-bill-terrible.

Reporters Without Borders. "Singapore's Foreign Interference Bill — Legal Monstrosity with Totalitarian Leanings." September 23, 2021. https://rsf.org/en/news/singapores-foreign-interference-bill-legal-monstrosity-totalitarian-leanings.

Robb, Amanda. "Anatomy of a Fake News Scandal." *Rolling Stone,* November 30, 2017. https://www.rollingstone.com/feature/anatomy-of-a-fake-news-scandal-125877/.

"Rohingya Sue Facebook for $150bn Over Myanmar Hate Speech." *BBC*, December 7, 2021. https://www.bbc.com/news/world-asia-59558090.

Robinson, John B. "Unlearning and Backcasting: Rethinking Some of the Questions We Ask About the Future." *Technological Forecasting and Social Change* 33, no. 4 (July 1988): 325–338.

Saba, Jennifer. "News Corp Sells Myspace, Ending Six-Year Saga." *Reuters*, June 30, 2011. https://www.reuters.com/article/us-newscorp-myspace-idUSTRE75S6D720110629.

Schultz, David and David L. Hudson. "Marketplace of Ideas." *The First Amendment Encyclopedia*, Middle Tennessee State University, 2017. https://www.mtsu.edu/first-amendment/article/999/marketplace-of-ideas.

Schwab, Klaus. "The Fourth Industrial Revolution: What It Means, How to Respond." *World Economic Forum*, January 14, 2016. https://www.weforum.org/agenda/2016/01/the-fourth-industrial-revolution-what-it-means-and-how-to-respond/.

Seneca, Lucius Annaeus. "On the Tranquility of the Mind." In *Oxford World's Classics: Seneca: Dialogues and Essays,* edited by John Davie and Tobias Reinhardt, 132. Oxford: Oxford University Press, 2007.

Seow, Peck Ngiam. "Nanyang Siang Pau." *Singapore Infopedia*, 2017. https://eresources.nlb.gov.sg/infopedia/articles/SIP_2017-01-10_095946.html.

Shafeeq, Syarafana. "ST Singaporean of the Year Nominee: Couple Offer Groceries to the Needy at Their Door." *The Straits Times,* November 1, 2021. https://www.straitstimes.com/singapore/couple-offer-groceries-to-the-needy-at-their-door.

Shanmugaratnam, Tharman. "Budget Statement 2008: Creating a Top Quality Economy, Building a Resilient Community." Delivered in Parliament on February 15, 2008. https://www.mof.gov.sg/docs/default-source/default-document-library/singapore-budget/budget-archives/2008/fy2008_budget_statement.pdf?sfvrsn=cbc23f72_2.

Shanmugaratnam, Tharman. "DPM Tharman Shanmugaratnam's Dialogue at the IPS 30th Anniversary Event." Edited Transcript of the Dialogue on October 25, 2018. https://www.pmo.gov.sg/Newsroom/dpm-tharmans-dialogue-ips-30th-anniversary-event.

Singapore Parliamentary Debates. Official Report (March 27, 1974) vol 33. (Jek Yeun Thong, Minister for Culture).

Singapore Press Holdings. "7 in 10 of Singapore Population Access SPH Content Properties Weekly, SPH Number 1 in Digital News: GfK Research." September 2, 2021. https://www.imsph.sg/7-in-10-of-singapore-population-access-sph-content-properties-weekly-sph-number-1-in-digital-news-gfk-research/.

Soon, Carol. "IPS Survey on Internet and Media Use During GE2020." October 8, 2020. https://lkyspp.nus.edu.sg/docs/default-source/ips/presentation-by-dr-carol-soon_ips-online-forum-on-internet-and-media-use-in-ge2020.pdf.

Statista. "Advertising Revenue of Google from 2001 to 2021." February 7, 2022. https://www.statista.com/statistics/266249/advertising-revenue-of-google/.

Statista. "Digital Economy Compass 2021." Accessed April 26, 2022. https://www.statista.com/study/105653/digital-economy-compass/.

Statista. "Estimated Cost of Digital Ad Fraud Worldwide." [2018–2023 data]. September 14, 2021. https://www.statista.com/statistics/677466/digital-ad-fraud-cost.

Stephen R. Covey. *The 7 Habits of Highly Effective People: 30th Anniversary Edition.* New York: Simon & Schuster, 2020.

Tan, Sue-Ann. "SPH Posts First Net Loss of $83.7 Million Amid the Covid-19 Pandemic." *The Straits Times*, October 13, 2020. https://www.straitstimes.com/business/companies-markets/sph-posts-first-net-loss-of-837-million-amid-the-coronavirus-pandemic.

Tan, Theresa. "Meet Singapore's Newer Philanthropic Foundations: They Give Millions, Seeking to Spark Social Change." *The Straits Times*, October 18, 2021. https://www.straitstimes.com/singapore/community/meet-spores-newer-philanthropic-foundations-they-give-millions-seeking-to-spark.

Teo, Josephine. "MCI Response to PQ on Update on Discussion with SPH Media Trust on Funding Support and Measures to Ensure Its Sustainability in Highly Competitive Media Industry and Limited Local Market." Transcript of speech delivered at Parliament Sitting on February 15, 2022. https://www.mci.gov.sg/pressroom/news-and-stories/pressroom/2022/2/mci-response-to-pq-on-update-on-discussion-with-sph-media-trust-on-funding-support-and-measures-to-ensure-its-sustainability-in-highly-competitive-media-industry-and-limited-local-market.

Tey, Tsun Hang. "Confining the Freedom of the Press in Singapore: A 'Pragmatic' Press for 'Nation-Building'?" *Human Rights Quarterly* 30, no. 4 (2008): 876–905.

The National Volunteer and Philanthropy Centre. "NVPC Celebrates the Generosity of Singapore With New Historic Milestone Surpassing $100M in Donations." April 13, 2021. https://cityofgood.sg/newsroom/nvpc-celebrates-the-generosity-of-singapore-with-new-historic-milestone-surpassing-100m-in-donations/.

"The Third Industrial Revolution." *The Economist*, April 21, 2012. https://www.economist.com/leaders/2012/04/21/the-third-industrial-revolution.

"Timeline of Computer History." Computer History Museum. Accessed August 25, 2022. https://www.computerhistory.org/timeline/.

Turnbull, Mary. *Dateline Singapore: 150 Years of the Straits Times*. Singapore: Times Editions, 1995.

United Nations. "International Convention on the Protection of the Rights of All Migrant Workers and Members of Their Families." Accessed May 6, 2022. https://www.ohchr.org/sites/default/files/cmw.pdf.

United Nations. "The 17 Goals." Accessed May 9, 2022. https://sdgs.un.org/goals.

United Nations. "Universal Declaration of Human Rights." Accessed April 14, 2022. https://www.un.org/en/about-us/universal-declaration-of-human-rights.

University of Oxford. "Bhutan's Gross National Happiness Index." Accessed May 9, 2022. https://ophi.org.uk/policy/gross-national-happiness-index/.

Wong, Lawrence. "Budget 2022 Speech — As Delivered." February 18, 2022. https://www.sgpc.gov.sg/sgpcmedia/media_releases/mof/press_release/P-20220218-3/attachment/Budget%202022%20Speech%20-%20As%20Delivered.pdf.

"World Wide Web vs Internet — What's the Difference?" *BBC*, March 11, 2019. https://www.bbc.co.uk/newsround/47523993.

Yahoo Finance. "Alphabet Inc." Accessed April 26, 2022. https://finance.yahoo.com/quote/GOOG/.

Yahoo Finance. "Amazon.com, Inc." Accessed April 26, 2022. https://finance.yahoo.com/quote/AMZN/.

"Young Girl Returned After Kidnapping by Man She Met on Roblox." *BBC*, March 3, 2022. https://www.bbc.com/news/world-us-canada-60607782.

Zhi Wei and Kartini Saparudin. "National Pledge." *Singapore Infopedia*, August 1, 2014. https://eresources.nlb.gov.sg/infopedia/articles/SIP_84_2004-12-13.html.

Index

A
advertising fraud, 60, 61, 63, 64
Alphabet, 54, 60
Amazon, 53, 54
America, 5
America Online, 27, 52
Apple, 60
artificial intelligence (AI), xiv, 94, 95, 97–99, 108
Australia, 73, 77

B
backcasting, 80–83, 93, 102
Bangladesh, 59
Berita Harian, 20, 23, 43
Bhutan, 92
big tech, 48, 55, 73
blockchain, 66, 67
broadcast, 2, 6, 10
Broadcasting Act, xiii, 10

C
Cheong Yip Seng, xi, 23, 24, 26
China, 55, 69, 72, 99
click fraud, 63
climate crisis, 93, 97
CNN, 50, 58
Commissioner of Charities, 91
COVID-19, 12, 31, 33, 110

D
Declaration of the Rights of Man, 4
Defamation Act, 11
desired future, 81–84, 90–99, 103
digital advertising, xiv, 57, 59–64
disinformation, 69
domain spoofing, 63
Donald Trump, 49, 56, 58
dot-com boom, 52, 53

dot-com bubble, 27
dot-coms, 52
Dr Lim Boon Keng, 16

E
Eastern Sun, 21
eBay, 53
Europe, 64, 82
European Convention on Human Rights, 4, 6

F
Facebook, 30, 31, 53–60, 96
fake news, 11, 33, 38, 49, 57, 69, 96, 105
Financial Times, xi, 63
Foreign Affairs, 58
Foreign Interference (Countermeasures) Act (FICA), 11, 15
fourth estate, 7, 107
fragmentation, 76
Francis Fukuyama, 58, 82
freedom of expression, 3–5
freedom of speech, 3–5

G
Global Commission on Internet Governance, 65
Goh Chok Tong, 40, 44
Google, 30, 31, 53–55, 60
government crackdowns, xiii, 21
Gross National Happiness Index, 92
Guardian, 58

H
happiness, 92, 93
Hillary Clinton, 49, 57
Hussein Jahidin, 23

I
inclusivity, 86, 93
Industrial Revolution, 50, 53
Instagram, 103
Internal Security Act, 11, 22, 23
International Labour Organization (ILO), 87
Internet, xiv, 15, 27, 29–31, 33, 48–50, 52–57, 59–62, 64–72, 74–76, 80, 95–97
Internet governance, 48, 64, 67, 78, 80

J
Janadas Devan, ix
JB Jeyaratnam, 24
Jek Yuen Thong, 10
Josephine Teo, 33, 34
journalism, 14, 24, 37, 43, 77, 98, 108, 109

K
Kishore Mahbubani, 32
Kuala Lumpur, 16–18

L
Lat Pau, 19
Lawrence Wong, 89
Lee Eu Seng, 22, 23
Lee Hsien Loong, xii, 40, 44
Lee Kuan Yew, x, xi, xiii, 2, 8, 10, 18, 20, 22, 23, 25–27, 36, 37, 40, 44
Lee Mau Seng, 22
legacy media, 48, 76, 77, 80, 105
Lianhe Wanbao, 19, 20
Lianhe Zaobao, 19, 99
Lim Kim San, 29
Lyndley Holloway, x, xi

M
Malaya Tribune, 16, 17
Malaysia, x, 18, 23
Maria Hertogh riots, 17, 18
marketplace of ideas, 6, 8, 12
Mediacorp, 26–28
media entrepreneurs, 77
media laws, 2, 6, 8, 10, 11, 14
Meta, 30, 60, 96
metaverse, 69, 95–97
Ming Pao, 20
minimum wage, 87, 88
Ministry of Communications and Information, 34
Ministry of Home Affairs, 74
Ministry of Manpower, 87
Ministry of Trade and Industry, 88
misinformation, 11, 33, 35, 56, 57, 59, 69, 105
Myanmar, 59

N
Nanyang Siang Pau, 19, 22, 25
National Volunteer and Philanthropy Centre (NVPC), 91
nation-building, 8, 12, 37, 38
net-zero, 93
new media, 48, 103
News Media and Digital Platforms Mandatory Bargaining Code, 73
newspaper, 8–10, 15, 17, 19, 22, 23, 25, 26, 28, 42, 104, 109
Newspaper and Printing Presses Act, xiii, 2, 8–10, 23, 41
New York Times, 32, 43, 63
Non-Fungible Token (NFT), 75, 96
North Atlantic Treaty Organization, 82

O
Official Secrets Act, 10
Ong Pang Boon, 84

open, secure, trustworthy and inclusive, 67, 71

P
People's Action Party (PAP), 8, 10, 14, 18, 21, 74
Peter Lim, x, xii, 25
philanthropy, 90, 91, 93
polarisation, 58, 59, 85, 106
press freedom, 2, 3, 6, 14, 40, 41
Protection from Online Falsehoods and Manipulation Act (POFMA), 11, 15, 64, 73
Pritam Singh, 34
propaganda, 10, 12, 33, 35, 38, 96

R
Ravi Menon, 86, 89
regulation, 55, 56, 64, 66, 69, 70, 72, 74, 75
Reporters Without Borders, 6, 14, 15, 40, 41
Reuters Digital News Report, 76
Roblox, 75, 96
Rupert Murdoch, 6, 9, 37
Russia, 82

S
Samad Ismail, 23
Section 230, 33, 55, 58
Section 377A, 85
Shamsuddin Tung, 22
Shin Min Daily News, 20, 25
Sin Chew Jit Poh, 19, 21, 25
Singapore, x, xiv, 4, 5, 8–11, 13–18, 20, 21, 23, 24, 27, 28, 32, 36, 37, 41, 45, 64, 67, 69, 71–74, 80, 82–85, 87, 88, 90, 91, 93, 95, 97–100, 103, 104
Singapore Armed Forces, 83
Singapore Chronicle, 15

Singapore Constitution, 4, 5, 8
Singapore Kindness Movement, 92
Singapore media, ix, xi, xii, xv, 2, 8, 11–15, 20, 21, 35, 36, 97
Singapore Monitor, 25
Singapore News and Publications Limited (SNPL), 25, 26
Singapore pledge, 83, 84
Singapore Press Holdings (SPH), xi–xiii, xv, 3, 11, 26–33, 43, 45, 107
Smart Nation Initiative, 65
Snapchat, 103
social media, 2, 49, 54, 76, 78, 105, 107
social mobility, 86, 93
SPH media, 29, 32, 33
SPH Media Trust (SMT), xii, xv, 3, 29, 33, 34, 41, 48, 76, 97–100, 103, 104, 106
S. Rajaratnam, 83, 92
S R Nathan, x, 25
Straits Times Press, x, 20, 25, 26
Streats, 28
subscription model, 43
Sustainable Development Goals, 93, 97

T
Tamil Murasu, 20
Tharman Shanmugaratnam, 86, 90
The Business Times, 29, 43, 83
The New Straits Times, 18
The Singapore Free Press, 16
The Singapore Herald, 22
The Straits Times (ST), ix–xiii, 2, 10, 16–18, 23, 24, 32, 38, 39, 42, 43, 76, 80, 91, 104, 107
TikTok, 103, 105
Tim Berners-Lee, 70
Time Warner, 27, 52

Tjong Yik Min, 29
Today, 28
Twitter, 56–58, 105

U
Ukraine, 82
United Nations (UN), 3, 5, 87, 93, 97
United States (US), x, 5–8, 27, 29, 30, 33, 37, 44, 49, 54, 55, 57, 58, 61, 64, 85, 96
Universal Declaration of Human Rights, 3
US Constitution, 3, 5
Utusan Malaysia, 20
Utusan Melayu, 20

V
Vivian Balakrishnan, 65, 70

W
wealth tax, 89, 90
Web 2.0, 52
Wee Kim Wee, 17, 18
WhatsApp, 103, 105
wilful misinformation, xiv, 49, 56–58, 96
workfare income supplement (WIS), 88, 89
World Press Freedom Index, 6, 14, 40
World Wide Web, 50, 55, 69, 70, 72

X
Xing Bao, 19

Z
Zaobao, 43

CPSIA information can be obtained
at www.ICGtesting.com
Printed in the USA
JSHW010813030423
39352JS00001B/135

9 789811 268304